NO OUTSIDERS IN OUR SCHOOL

Teaching the Equality Act in Primary Schools

ANDREW MOFFAT

First published 2016 by Speechmark Publishing Ltd.

Published 2017 by Routledge
2 Park Square, Milton Park, Abingdon, Oxon OX14 4RN
711 Third Avenue, New York, NY 10017, USA

Routledge is an imprint of the Taylor & Francis Group, an informa business

British Library Cataloguing in Publication Data
A catalogue record for this book is available from the British Library

ISBN 9781909301726 (pbk)
Printed and bound by CPI Group (UK) Ltd, Croydon, CR0 4YY

Contents

List of figures

List of tables

Preface

The Equality Act 2010 states that it is against the law to discriminate against anyone because of:

- age

- disability

- gender reassignment

- marriage and civil partnership

- pregnancy or maternity

- race

- religion or belief

- sex

- sexual orientation.

(Government, 2010, p1)

The website www.equalitiesprimary.com links to news, new books and other useful resources including updated lesson plans for teaching the Equality Act 2010 in primary schools.

Please contact andy@equalitiesprimary.com for advice or training.

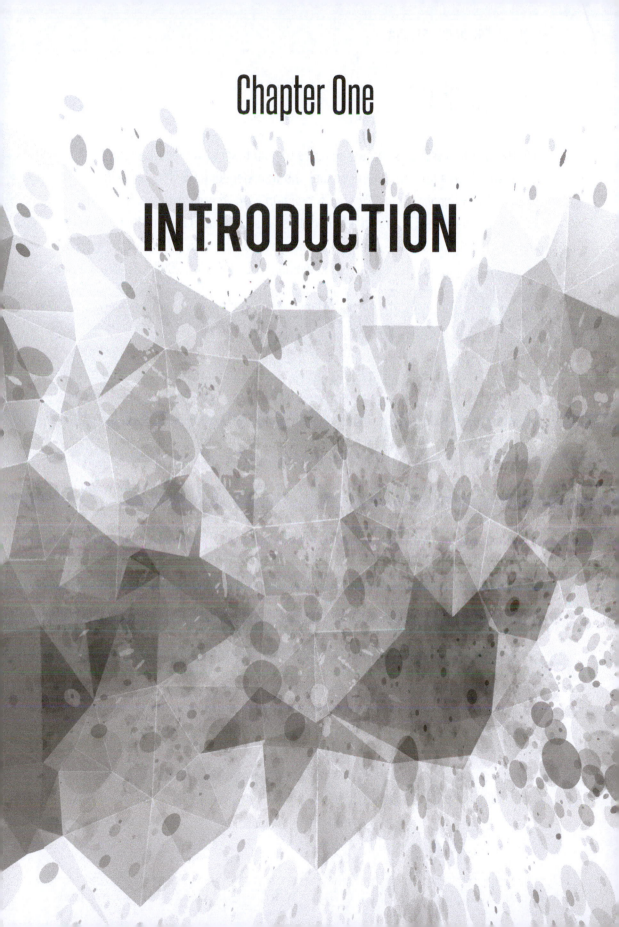

Chapter One

INTRODUCTION

Introduction

In 2007 I wrote a sequence of lesson plans to help teachers deliver lessons on equality with a lesbian, gay, bi-sexual and transgender (LGBT) focus, called *Challenging Homophobia in Primary Schools: An Early Years Resource.* Since then I have continually rewritten and adapted these resources and taught the lessons in many different schools. The opening line of the resource was, 'We need to teach five year olds that gay and lesbian men and women exist' (Moffat, 2007, p1). We are nine years further in to the new century and I am overjoyed to say that I've changed my mind about this first line.

Eight years on, I don't believe that we need to be teaching children that gay men and lesbian women exist because children know that already. Any child who has a television has seen a gay couple or a gay character. Any child living in a family, in contact with uncles, aunts, cousins, stepbrothers and stepsisters, or in a street where neighbours talk to one another, is going to have been in contact with a gay person. What we now need to be teaching is that homophobia once existed but we don't have it in our school today, and that to be a person who is gay or lesbian or transgender or bi-sexual is normal, acceptable and OK. Children also need to be learning that they may identify or may not identify as LGBT as they grow up, and that whoever they grow into as an adult is also perfectly normal and acceptable.

Another shift for me since 2007 is in the particular way in which I deliver this work in my school. No longer should we separate LGBT education from education about other equalities; equality is best taught in the context of British law, where all protected characteristics of the Equality Act 2010 are included in a curriculum that celebrates difference. So not only are people of different sexual orientations welcome in our primary school, people of different ethnicities, genders, gender identities, religions, ages and abilities are also most welcome. There are no outsiders in our school; to quote the South African social rights activist Desmond Tutu (2004), 'Everyone is an insider, no matter their beliefs, whatever their colour, gender or sexuality' (No Outsiders Project Team, 2010, pix).

I am not the only one to have changed since 2007; the law around this work has shifted dramatically in eight years: we now have legal gay marriages across the UK and Ireland, for example. In fact, Ireland became the first country to hold a referendum on equal gay marriage in 2015 and the 'Yes' vote signalled more than ever the public perception on equalities. The Equality Act 2010 makes it quite clear that discrimination is not to be tolerated in society and we now have Ofsted asking schools to demonstrate how they are tackling homophobic bullying, teaching about different families and promoting British values.

However, at the same time, we have a perceived worrying rise in the radicalisation of young people and there is currently little clear guidance on how schools can meet the needs of children who are hearing different messages outside the school walls to the messages of equality that they hear inside. The election campaign of 2015 featured an interesting dialogue between the British Labour MP Tristram Hunt and a schoolboy, as reported by *The Independent* newspaper:

> *'Do you know who you'd vote for?' asked the man hoping to become the next Education Secretary.*
> *'Ukip,' came the response from the schoolboy.*
> *'You'd vote Ukip? Very good,' a panicked Mr Hunt replied.*
> *'Why's that?'*
> *'It might get all the foreigners out,' the kid explained.*
>
> (Dathan, 2015, n.p.)

At the time, this was seen as an embarrassing blunder for a Labour MP on the campaign trail, but of course for educators it also demonstrates the presence of ideas in schools that we don't want to hear. How can we ensure that these ideas are not the accepted norm on the playground? We can't be simply telling children that their beliefs are wrong or unacceptable; we have to be delivering a curriculum that enables children to understand the benefits that exist in a society where diversity and difference are celebrated. Furthermore, we need our children to want to be part of that society, and we have to sell it to them; that desire may not come naturally by itself.

In conclusion, the aim of this resource is to provide teachers with a curriculum that promotes equality for all sections of the community. But more than that, this resource aims to bring children and parents or carers (hereafter referred to as 'parents') on board from the start so that children leave our primary schools happy and excited about living in a community full of difference and diversity, whether that is through ethnicity, gender, ability, sexual orientation, gender identity, age or religion. Children must be excited about living in a diverse twenty-first century, and want to keep it like that – not fight against it.

Acknowlegements

The 'no outsiders' quote by Desmond Tutu formed the basis for a project that ran from 2006 to 2008, supporting primary teachers to develop strategies to address lesbian, gay, bi-sexual and transgender equality in primary schools. The 'no outsiders' project was funded by the Economic and Social Research Council (ESRC) and paved the way for this resource. Most of the ideas in this resource originated within those two years and I would like to thank that fantastic and brave team for starting me on my journey.

I also want to thank Hazel Pulley at Parkfield Community School in Birmingham and the school staff team for being so brilliant, Mark Jenett for being so full of good advice and Annie Hargreaves for giving me the idea in the first place. Also thanks to David for being so supportive.

Ｒ Routledge
Taylor & Francis Group

Chapter Two

PREPARING YOUR PATH – CREATING THE WHOLE-SCHOOL ETHOS

Preparing your path – creating the whole-school ethos

One of the main things I have learned from the three schools where I have delivered this resource is to ensure that work on equalities is embedded across the school. For this work to succeed, there needs to be a whole-school ethos to which everyone signs up.

How do we create an ethos?

Governors

First, the governors need to be on board. Transparency is critical and the school leadership team (SLT) needs to be clear about the vision and aims in order to take it to the governors. Take a copy about this resource, and all the books it makes reference to, to a governors' meeting and give everyone half an hour to read the texts. In my current school some governors borrowed books to take home and read in detail, in order to be confident about the proposals. Be clear that we are not asking for governors' permission to do this work; the government is already asking schools to promote equality and diversity, and Ofsted is judging schools on the strategies they are using. But, at the same time, we do need our governing bodies to be moving with us and in full understanding of our aims and expectations.

Staff training

Once the governors have been informed of the vision, aims and proposals, staff training is essential to ensure that all staff (including teaching assistants (TAs) and lunch-time supervisors) have the skills to deliver the messages we are promoting. We need a common language to be used by all staff across the school and on the playground to challenge any discrimination or prejudicial behaviour that arises and to promote the vision we are creating.

R Routledge
Taylor & Francis Group

Of course, some staff may not feel comfortable with some of the messages. It is unlikely that anyone will have tensions arising from saying to children that a person who uses a wheelchair or hearing aid is welcome at the school, but a person's faith may provide a tension with saying that it is OK to be gay. This is where the Equality Act 2010 is helpful. It clearly states:

The public sector Equality Duty came into force across Great Britain on 5 April 2011. It means that public bodies have to consider all individuals when carrying out their day-to-day work – in shaping policy, in delivering services and in relation to their own employees.

It also requires that public bodies:

- have due regard to the need to eliminate discrimination
- advance equality of opportunity
- foster good relations between different people when carrying out their activities.

(Government Equalities Office, 2013, p1)

The wording of this makes it plain to public bodies (ie schools) that promoting some of the protected characteristics of the Equality Act while ignoring others is simply against UK law. So we cannot promote an ethos where people of diverse faith are welcome but people of diverse sexual orientation are not. Similarly, children need to be taught that this is the law, as when children eventually leave school and get a job, they will not stay employed for long if they say to black colleagues, 'I am racist, so I don't want to work with you!' or to gay colleagues, 'As my faith says homosexuality is a sin, I don't want to work with you.'

The lesson plans in this resource are all based on children's picture books, and I have aimed to make them as accessible as possible for following and delivering. Hold a staff meeting and give out the books for everyone to read. Try out the role plays and games and have the discussions around challenging potential questions (see Chapter 5 'Simple answers to challenging questions'). By far the most effective schools are those that have taken these plans and made them their own. Some schools teach these lessons as one-offs during personal, social, health and economic education (PSHE), while some spend a whole week on a text in literacy lessons, teasing out language and developing inference skills. Both strategies work; it's the way in which the school embraces the ethos that is critical rather than individual lessons. My advice is to identify a senior staff member to be responsible for overseeing the delivery of this resource and to monitor the delivery and whether the aims are being met throughout the school year.

Schools may want to lead their own training or there are many trainers available around the country who will happily come in for a half-day or a staff inset day. Some trainers will use their own materials, but the messages will be consistent, so it doesn't really matter which plans you use as long as your ethos is clear. It is very useful to have open discussions in staff meetings, particularly if some staff are uncomfortable with some of the messages, but keep in mind that opting out of the ethos is not an option for staff; we can have the discussion but the bottom line is that UK law says that schools need to promote equality of opportunity and that includes all equality.

Making the message clear

Mission statement

As visitors enter the school building there needs to be some signal that here is a school that promotes diversity: we are a place where everyone is welcome and all difference is celebrated. A mission statement makes the school ethos clear and also needs to include reference to behaviour that is not acceptable, that is, discrimination and bullying.

The Parkfield Community School mission statement (see Figure 2.1) is put up around the school so that the message is loud and clear.

Celebrating Diversity

Parkfield Community School endeavours to improve the lives of children, young people and families. We celebrate our rich diversity and take steps to prevent and tackle all kinds of bullying, including homophobic bullying. In doing so, we believe that children will attain more at school and our community will be happier and more successful.

We celebrate all our children and their families without discrimination.

Figure 2.1: Parkfield Community School's mission statement

Signing-in to school

All schools have a signing-in system. Some signing-in is simply a book where you clock in and clock out; other systems demand that you agree to a conduct of behaviour. At my current school, as visitors sign in they are asked to read and agree to a visitor agreement (see Figure 2.2).

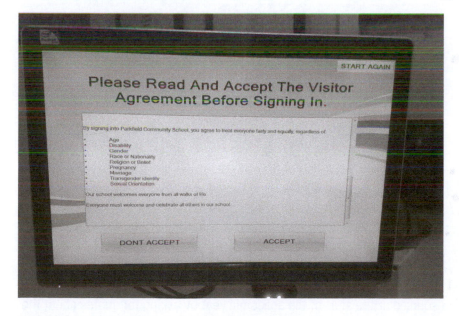

Figure 2.2: Parkfield Community School's signing-in system

This makes clear where the school stands on discrimination and equalities: regardless of your opinion on equalities, if you want to come in here, you sign up to ours; after all, we are following the guidelines set out in British law.

Equality Act posters
We have Equality Act posters (see Figure 2.3) on every outside wall so that when parents collect their children they see the posters every day.

Figure 2.3: Parkfield Community School's Equality Act poster

There are six posters in total – each in weatherproof casing – around the school perimeter. The wording is simple and to the point and again makes quite clear that we protect all equalities at our school. Around each poster I have quotes from Year 6 pupils that I sourced at the start of the academic year by asking for quotes about the Equality Act.

Ⓡ Routledge
Taylor & Francis Group

Among these quotes are:

'Respect each other. Don't be racist. Everyone is equal.'

'No matter what colour you are, you are welcome here.'

'Everybody is equal due to the Equality Act.'

'We respect each other's gender and if you are gay or straight.'

'We respect everyone's religion and gender.'

'Do not judge people by the colour of their skin.'

'I believe that having no outsiders is a great thing because no one should be left out.'

The quotes stay up all year and will be replaced by new Year 6 quotes at the start of the next academic year.

Displays around school

Children need to be surrounded by a consistent message: there are no outsiders here; everyone is different; we like being different; we are all equal in our difference; I can get along with you even though we are different; we live in the UK and the law says this.

Many children's books that support a message of difference provide a great stimulus for classroom displays; some are included in this resource, for example *This is Our House* by Michael Rosen (2007).

At a previous school I asked every child to draw a self-portrait on a postage-size stamp, stuck them up under a 'This is our school' banner, asked Year 6 to name the groups of people who were welcome at our school – black, white, people who wear glasses, Asian, Irish, gay, ginger hair, female, male, and so on – and then asked them to put those groups up under the subheading 'Everyone is welcome at our school'.

Figure 2.4 shows a simple lesson that was delivered by the Early Years Foundation Stage (EYFS) team at my current school using *Red Rockets and Rainbow Jelly* by Sue Heap and Nick Sharrat (2003).

Routledge
Taylor & Francis Group

Figure 2.4: Parkfield Community School's 'We all like …' and 'Some of us like …' displays

The Early Years children also added their own quotes to the equalities poster outside their entrance rather than use quotes by Year 6. The quotes read, 'There are no outsiders', 'We are all different and that is OK', 'We are all friends' and 'We like different things and that is OK'.

Figure 2.5 shows a display created by a Year 2 class who used *The Other Ark* by Lynley Dodd (2006) to create a display about making sure that no one is left out despite each of us being different.

Figure 2.5: Parkfield Community School's 'No outsiders' display

Ⓡ Routledge Taylor & Francis Group

Figure 2.6 shows the display in our pastoral care room that uses *It's Okay to Be Different* by Todd Parr (2009) to promote an acceptance of difference. If children are sent to us following an altercation, we add a new 'It's okay to …' so that the reminder is always there.

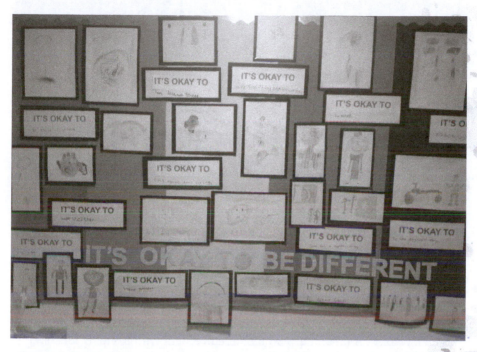

Figure 2.6: Parkfield Community School's 'It's okay to be different …' display

The display in Figure 2.7 (overleaf) promotes British values and includes reference to aspects of living in Britain that we want our children to celebrate. Our school has a cohort that is 98.8 per cent Muslim, so the vast majority of our children do not celebrate Christmas, but Christmas is a British celebration and we live in Britain so we had a Christmas card postbox and gave children the option to send cards to one another. We visit a Church of England (C of E) school regularly and joined them for Easter celebrations and a nativity in their church and we cooked traditional English and Asian dishes with them. These are all activities that schools have been doing for years and it's nothing new; however, we make an effort to publicise and promote the activities everywhere around school so that the ethos touches everyone.

Figure 2.7: Parkfield Community School's promotion of British values display

One photograph on the display features the retired Welsh professional rugby player Gareth Thomas, who we arranged to visit us through a deal with a supply teaching agency. I asked Gareth to play rugby with the children all afternoon and then to come out as homosexual in an assembly later that day. This worked incredibly well (see Chapter 6 'Coming out in primary schools') and the paragraph next to the photo of Gareth with Year 5 reads: 'Gareth Thomas visited and played rugby with Year 5. He told us he is gay and feels welcome at Parkfield Community School.'

There is another photograph showing a Christian mission group in an assembly with a display of artwork showing a bible story. I asked a child to write a note about listening to a Christian bible story as a Muslim and to justify why learning about other religions is important. The child wrote: 'It's OK for Muslim children to listen to a Christian assembly because it won't hurt you and it won't affect your religion. It's important to have a Christian assembly because you can learn about other things around the world.'

We have a 'Learning to be safe together' display in the main corridor. Our school also follows the Prevent agenda, which aims to stop the radicalisation of children and young people.

We asked children around the school to fill in details about their likes and dislikes, ethnicity, family details and experiences of different families to show the wealth of diversity around school despite most children following the same faith. Each child completed a form during an information and communications technology (ICT) lesson and imported a photograph. The forms are up for the year and will be replaced next year.

Also on the board there is a reference to the Equality Act. A child was asked to describe what the Act meant for our school and the resulting note was: 'All groups are welcome at Parkfield School. If you are black, white, Christian, Muslim, gay. We are all treated equally.'

The Equality Act should be referenced as much as possible to remind children and the community that equality is British law.

Reward the ethos

We have 'No outsiders' stickers that midday supervisors give out to children who are demonstrating behaviour on the playground that promotes the ethos, that is, making sure children are not left out and that there is no name calling or discrimination.

There is also a 'No outsiders' certificate, designed by a child in the school, which is used to promote the desired behaviour.

Support from the local authority

It made a huge difference to the work at Parkfield School to be able to say that the same work was being done in schools across the city, and indeed the country. In March 2015, Birmingham City Council sent out a letter to all head teachers and chairs of governors in which they stated: 'We expect that all schools in Birmingham will prevent and tackle homophobic, biophobic and transphobic bullying and language and talk about different family models.'

This was a wonderful green light that demonstrated to any parents concerned about our plans that we were not alone in doing this work. The resource I wrote in 2007 was now a full primary school pack including lesson plans from Reception to Year 6. Every school that takes on the lesson plans makes the journey easier for the next, as schools realise that they are not alone, and furthermore that there is a danger that they will be left behind if they are not promoting equalities in their curriculum.

Rehearse difficult conversations

The head teacher and I are aware that for some members of our community this work presents a tension, and we rehearse difficult conversations before meetings. In this way we are prepared for what may arise and unflustered if and when it does. I recommend sitting with the Senior Leadership Team and doing a 'worst-questions' scenario discussion where answers to potential questions are planned. This strategy has been a huge help to us in the last year. Some suggestions for questions to discuss are included in Chapter 5.

R Routledge
Taylor & Francis Group

Chapter Three

ASSEMBLIES – CREATING THE WHOLE-SCHOOL ETHOS

Assemblies – creating the whole-school ethos

We promote the school ethos every day in school assemblies. We run our assemblies using the following guidelines.

As the children come in, we have songs playing that are sung using a different language to English. We have a huge world map and the first thing we do to open the assembly is use a pointer stick to find the country where the music came from. The songs are not traditional music from that country; the aim is to show that music of all genres comes from countries all over the world and people in Bulgaria may well be listening to the same type of music as we are, yet in a different language. I tend to use a lot of ballads from the Eurovision Song Contest!

Often there are positive messages in the songs that I can highlight. We have a small display in the hall (two A3-sized papers) each week with details of what the song is and where it comes from as well as a brief synopsis of either the lyric content or the singer.

While the song is playing as children enter the hall, we have an image on the whiteboard at the front. Every week I select images from *The Guardian* online 'Photo highlights of the day' to show in assemblies. Links to examples of photos I use in my assemblies can be found at www.equalitiesprimary.com (Moffat, 2015). These are photographs taken from around the world in the last 24 hours. Some are from news stories. Some are from events. Often there are random photographs of people going about their daily lives in a country far away. We spend two minutes talking about the picture – exploring where the children think it was taken, what they think it is showing and why they believe the photographer chose to take that particular photograph. Then we find the place where the photo was taken on the world map. The aim is to bring the wide world into the assembly every day; we are promoting interest in the world around us because we are part of that world.

R Routledge
Taylor & Francis Group

When there are relevant news stories, the photos are a great way to stimulate discussion. For example, after the *Charlie Hebdo* attacks in France in January 2015 there was a photo I used in a Year 5 and 6 assembly of Muslim women on a peace march in Paris holding placards with the word 'peace' written on them in Arabic. One placard read, 'I am Muslim, not a terrorist.' This was a superb stimulus for discussion: Why is she holding that placard? What does she want people to understand?

Following the referendum on gay marriage in Ireland later that year, I used a photo in Key Stage 2 assemblies showing a large demonstration in Dublin where everyone was holding up an 'Equality' sign. Discussion revolved around questions such as: Why? What's happening? What does it mean for us? Do we have gay marriage in the UK?

The stories we read in assemblies are all taken from this resource (Chapter 7) or from an emotional literacy scheme of work which I wrote a few years ago (Moffat 2012). The picture books all focus on emotional well-being or recognition of feelings. I tend to use one set of books for Key Stage 1 assemblies and another for Key Stage 2 assemblies. Each book provides opportunities for relating the situation to real life: What would you do? How is the character feeling? What do you think of the ending? What is the message in this book?

Chapter Four

ENGAGING PARENTS – LESSONS LEARNED FROM THREE SCHOOLS

Engaging parents – lessons learned from three schools

Delivering a scheme of work that challenges homophobia

It is unlikely that parents will be worried about the school teaching children that people in our community are differently abled. I have never had parents complain about lesson plans that challenge gender stereotypes and sexism or lessons that talk about people of different ages.

Challenging homophobia, in my experience, is an area where potential tensions can arise from some parents in a school. Parents may believe that their children are too young to learn about sexual orientation or may be aligned to a faith that identifies homosexuality as a lifestyle choice that is unacceptable.

Many schools will be able to do work around lesbian, gay, bi-sexual and transgender (LGBT) people without challenge or question and many are doing the work successfully today. However, for some schools, for a variety of reasons, teaching children that it's OK to be gay may present challenges. For this reason I am going to concentrate in this chapter on the potential obstacles that some schools may face using books in this resource that challenge homophobia. Of course, the strategies I am using to challenge homophobia can also be used to challenge attitudes towards ethnicity in different areas.

Successful implementation: lessons learned from one school

I have delivered this scheme of work in three schools since 2006 and as a member of the Senior Leadership Team in all settings. The first school where I used this resource was in Coventry, in a school on an estate where the British National Party (BNP) was consistently (at the time) coming second in local elections. At the time, the school had a predominantly white British cohort and we made a lot of effort to

Routledge Taylor & Francis Group

use resources in school to promote other cultures and ethnicities. I recall one child in Year 5 once saying to me, 'I don't believe in black people', which I found astonishing but at the same time an indication of how vital this work was.

All of this experience made me nervous about starting work to challenge homophobia because I assumed that there would be a negative response from parents who were unhappy about picture books with a focus on gay and lesbian people. We decided to be open and transparent from the beginning and held year group meetings (the school had one class in each year group) to show the books and explain the aims of the project. I felt at the time that parents were genuinely grateful for our openness and honesty and I learned not to be so judgemental of parents whom I assumed would be homophobic, but actually weren't at all!

The work at that first school went extremely well and I remained at the school for a further three years, coming out to children and parents along the way. In that time the school received no complaints around challenging homophobia. In retrospect I feel the reasons it worked so well at that school were as follows:

- The school was settled and on an upward trajectory: results were improving, parents were generally happy and the head teacher was established and well thought of in the community.

- Before I came out to the children and parents, I had worked at the school for six years and was well known; I would stand on the playground every morning greeting parents and everyone knew me.

- The govenors were informed and on board from the beginning.

- We held a staff meeting before starting the work so that everyone had a chance to air concerns and ask questions and we created a common language so that all members of staff responded to children's comments in the same way.

Unsuccessful implementation: lessons learned from one school

The work was so successful at that first school that I felt that I could work in any setting and get the same response. In 2009, I moved to a school in Birmingham where the cohort was more ethnically mixed with the two largest communities being African-Caribbean and Somali Muslim.

I spent the first year at the school preparing my path; I introduced an ethos around 'no outsiders' where everyone was welcome and set up an emotional literacy curriculum using picture books to teach about feelings and citizenship. By the end of the summer term I requested a governors' meeting to introduce the *Challenging Homophobia* resource and explain how I wanted to make it work at the school.

Unfortunately, at the meeting I was unable to convince the governors and the head teacher to begin teaching the resource and the message was to put the work on hold. At the time I was unsure how to proceed, so I spent the next couple of years gradually dropping the texts that challenged homophobia into the curriculum and becoming more and more confident with each term that passed without complaint. However, the failure to achieve a positive signal from the governors was a huge error on my part, as it meant that when there was a complaint further down the line, there was no back-up for me.

Today, it would be very difficult for a governing body to turn down a request to embark on a scheme to challenge homophobia because the law in the UK has changed. In 2010, Ofsted was not judging schools on how they were teaching about different families and the Equality Act was yet to have an impact; there was a sense that some schools were making a choice to do this work, but there was little encouragement from government.

Ironically, the work in school at the time was proving to be very successful; children were signing up to the 'no outsiders' ethos and the books were being used. However, there was nothing written down; there was no policy or statement to show our intent. So, officially, we weren't doing the work; we certainly weren't having discussions with the parents about doing it.

I decided after being at the school for four years to come out to the children, so I did that in an assembly when I showed a poster made by Year 6 pupils about the book *King and King*. There was little response from parents at first but unfortunately immediately after that there was a sudden period of transition where the head teacher left and a new head took over who was unknown to the parents.

At exactly that time one of the Year 5 classes started a week of lessons on the text *And Tango Makes Three* (a true story about two male penguins in a zoo which fall in love and raise a chick together), focusing on the authors' viewpoint as well as using the text to teach about grammar and punctuation. After the first lesson there was a letter of complaint from a parent to say that his son was being taught Sex and Relationship Education (SRE), specifically about gay people, and he wanted to remove the child from future lessons referring to the *And Tango Makes Three* text.

At this point the decisions I had made two years ago caught up with me; as there was no diversity statement, no governor rubber stamp and no policy for challenging homophobia, the work appeared to be isolated and led solely by me. Word spread around the playground that the school was teaching gay lessons and that I had a gay agenda. A heated meeting was held to which 40 parents came to say that I had no business coming out to children and that all lessons focusing on LGBT people should be removed from the curriculum.

I decided that this was a fight I was not going to win and, furthermore, that there were more important battles for the school at the time, so I immediately looked for another job and was able to resign and leave by the end of the following term.

There were harsh lessons to be learned from my experience at this school.

- It is vital to have governor support from the beginning. With no back-up from governors when the complaints came in, I was isolated and, more importantly, the work was isolated and seen as something that only I was promoting.

- The head teacher should be leading and modelling the ethos from the top down. The work needs to be part of a whole-school ethos.

Routledge
Taylor & Francis Group

- Parents need to be told that the work is going on; this curriculum must not be a surprise for them. Parents need to see and read the picture books and have the ethos explained: that this is not sex education, rather it is about promoting diversity and celebrating difference. There is the argument that by raising the subject we are creating an issue that doesn't need to be there. But the alternative is to risk being accused of having an agenda and hiding a curriculum, which is the last thing that a school wants. There will be some schools where this really will not be a tension, but regardless the parents still need to be informed.

- All members of staff need to be doing the work. Everyone has to sign up; we can't have children getting the message that Mrs Smith is OK with gay people but Mrs Jones isn't OK. The section concerned with personal and professional conduct in the Teachers' Standards says:

> **Teachers uphold public trust in the profession and maintain high standards of ethics and behaviour, within and outside school, by ... not undermining fundamental British values, including democracy, the rule of law, individual liberty and mutual respect, and tolerance of those with different faiths and beliefs.**
>
> (Department for Education, 2011, p1)

Outside school, teachers may hold a view that homosexuality is wrong, but part of a teacher's job today is to uphold British values and British law, and in British law a person cannot face discrimination because of their race, religion, gender identity, age, disability, gender or sexual orientation. Schools, which are public bodies, need to follow the guidance from the Equality Act 2010; we are all responsible for promoting diversity and celebrating difference, which includes equality for LGBT people.

There were many parents who approached me in my final days at the school to express their concern that I wasn't leaving 'because of the gay stuff'. One parent told me that she didn't care if her doctor was gay and it made no difference to her whether I was gay, too. I was reminded once again that it really was not the case that the community was a homophobic one; there were pockets of homophobic

Routledge
Taylor & Francis Group

behaviour but the majority of parents were happy to have their children growing up knowing that there are different people in their community, including people who were LGBT.

Successful implementation: lessons learned from one school

I moved to another school on the other side of Birmingham which had a cohort that was 98 per cent Muslim because I still wanted to prove that this work could be successful in every school. I was open with the head teacher about what had happened previously and what I had learned from both experiences. We worked very hard to ensure that whatever we did at this school was going to result in a very different conclusion.

Outline of steps taken to make the work a success

The following is an outline of the steps we took to make this work a success.

2014

May: The diversity statement is in place (see Chapter 2): framed in the entrance, on the wall around school and on the website.

The school is recording homophobic incidents alongside incidents of racism. These are collated every term, analysed and parents are notified.

July: Before taking any further steps, I am invited to lead a governors meeting to explain the resource and show all the books we want to use. The governors take the time to read all of the texts and some take them home to re-read.

While not all of the governors are 100 per cent comfortable with teaching about homosexuality in school, even in the context of the Equality Act 2010, all recognise the statutory duty that the school has to promote equalities and tackle discrimination and potential homophobic bullying. The governors agree to support the work, beginning across the school from September.

We check that all of our relevant policies include reference to challenging homophobia within the equalities framework. This includes the Anti Bullying Policy, PSHE and Citizenship Policy, Inclusion Policy, Gender Equality Policy.

September: On the first day back, we hold an afternoon staff meeting on challenging homophobia where all staff (including midday supervisors and teaching assistants) read the books and take part in role plays detailed on the lesson plans. The head teacher explains that these lessons are a compulsory part of our curriculum and that they support the school ethos, which in turn is supported by the governors. As part of the training, we identify common language and definitions for 'gay' and 'lesbian' so that if a child asks about the meaning of one of these terms, or uses either word in a negative way, we are all coming back with the same response: 'gay' means when two men love each other and 'lesbian' means when two women love each other, and that's OK – there are no outsiders at our school and we welcome everyone.

The first assemblies of the new academic year are led by the head teacher who shows a picture of the Houses of Parliament and talks about the Equality Act 2010 and how it affects us. She is quite clear to the children that *everyone* is welcome in our school. She says that, in our school, if you are black then you are welcome, if you are white then you are welcome, if you are a girl then you are welcome, if you are gay or lesbian then you are welcome and if you are Muslim then you are welcome.

The following message is delivered: 'We respect one another's race, religion, gender identity, age, disabilities, sexual orientation and gender.' Posters delivering this message are put up around school and in classes. Teachers make sure that children know what the different characteristics mean and why we say that everyone is welcome. Year 6 children write statements about the Equality Act. These are put up around the four posters that are on the outside walls of the school.

A letter is sent to parents – one year group at a time – inviting them in to look at the books we are using to challenge homophobia. We tell the parents that the books are teaching children about different families and sexual orientations. In the whole school only one parent attends. At first this parent tells us that he does not want his child learning 'about gays' but after the head teacher and I put the work in the context of equalities and show him the books, he leaves happier.

R Routledge Taylor & Francis Group

September 2014–February 2015: Children are taught lessons from the resource as part of teaching emotional literacy. A different text is used every week, and we focus on a different module every half-term: Pupil Voice; Safe and Unsafe; Needed and Lonely; Excited and Scared; Kind and Selfish; Shy, Confident and Proud; and Transition (the curriculum being based on Moffat, 2012). The books used in this resource, including those dealing with challenging homophobia, are dropped in throughout the year.

November: The Society for the Protection of Unborn Children (SPUC) attempts to hold a meeting in Birmingham about the *Challenging Homophobia in Primary Schools* (CHIPS) resource (the original version of this resource) that our school and others in Birmingham are using. SPUC argues that the resource is putting children at risk. The meeting is later cancelled after we inform the venue about the purpose of the meeting.

There is suddenly a surge in complaints to the school about challenging homophobia. Some parents call for a public meeting at school to discuss the 'gay lessons'. We offer to see parents individually but only one parent takes up our offer. We show her the books and explain the lessons.

We continue with the work in school as normal.

December: We plan to hold parents evening as normal, but we are aware that some parents may ask teachers about the challenging homophobia lessons, so we prepare a statement for teachers to read out to parents if they are challenged, thus removing the risk of any teachers feeling unsure about how to respond to difficult questions. The statement reads: 'At our school we teach that there are no outsiders and that includes people who are gay. This is in line with British law and the Equality Act 2010 and also guidance from Birmingham City Council. Please visit our website to see what we teach. Any further questions please make an appointment to see the Head Teacher.'

2015

January: We set up an after-school club – Ambassadors Club – once a week to promote our 'no outsiders' ethos around Birmingham and also to enable our children to meet and mix with children from different cultures and with different experiences. We have focused on Year 5 children, and we take a small group to visit other schools for an hour after school where we play circle-time games and then geographical board games and card games before signing a handprint sheet to say that we are different and we attend different schools in different areas of the city but we get along. This is also a response to the Prevent agenda; we are teaching our children that they can get along with anyone, no matter who they are or where they live or what faith they follow.

February: SPUC attempts to hold another meeting in Birmingham. This time there is a marked increase in the numbers of complaints to the school about the 'gay lessons', so we decide to hold meetings for parents a class at a time, starting in Year 1 and moving up the school over the next two months. This means a total of 21 meetings, all attended by the head teacher and myself but, in the interests of the well-being of the school, we feel that it has become a priority. (See the parent letter invite in the Appendix.) The SPUC meeting is cancelled again after having to change venue three times. This presents a strong message: no venue in the city is willing to hold a meeting supporting homophobic views!

February–April: Parent meetings. A total of seven parents attend the Year 1 meetings, so we decide that, contrary to our expectations, most parents are not worried about this issue and will not be coming to meet us. From Year 2 upwards we hold one meeting per year group (however, if ten parents had turned up each day we would have kept the meetings to a class at a time).

At each meeting we begin by talking about the Equality Act 2010 and what it means for schools. We then show all of the books we are using, starting with those in Reception and moving gradually up to Year 6. We read all of the books to the parents and explain what the message is and how we are going to use it in the lesson. Each meeting is held in the last half hour of the school day.

Some parents at the meetings tell us that they are very concerned that, by reading the books, we are going to make their children gay. We tell them a child cannot be turned gay (we visited a Sikh temple last month and no child came back converted). Parents tell us they have been told we are showing gay and lesbian sex videos and we show them the books to demonstrate that that is not the case. We make it clear that the governors have approved all of the lessons and they will be going ahead. Parents are not able to remove their children from these lessons as they are not part of Sex and Relationship Education.

Some of the parents ask to be told when the next challenging homophobia lesson will be taking place so that they can come in and observe. We say that it is not our policy to have parents observe lessons. We also make the point that challenging homophobia is taught as part of celebrating diversity every day, all around school – in assemblies and on displays. It is simply not possible to remove a child from the school ethos.

To each meeting we get from four to nine parents. At every meeting there are parents telling us they are unhappy with our teaching that homosexuality is acceptable because Islam says it is not acceptable. We say we understand there is a tension here and we are not telling children what to think: we are simply preparing the children for life in Britain so that they grow up to have a rounded view of society and understand there are different people and communities where they live. We want our children to be able to work alongside anyone as they grow older without prejudice or fear.

At one meeting two mothers in full burqas argue about the rights and wrongs of the school teaching that it's OK to be gay. One says, 'If you want to live here and wear your veil you have to accept that schools are teaching about gay people. Go and live in Holland if you don't like it, where you can't wear this!' She grabs her veil. 'I choose to live in Britain because I can follow my faith and wear this.'

The meetings are challenging because some parents are visibly unhappy with what the school is trying to do. There is an air of resignation around some of the meetings where parents understand that this is British law and they are going to have to accept it. One mother tells us, 'You can say what you like at school but when my son gets home I will tell him the truth: that homosexuality is wrong.'

However, not all parents are unhappy. Many parents, particularly once they have read the books and seen that we are not talking about sex, leave happy with what we are doing. One father, after appearing very defensive at the start, leaves saying, 'You have my blessing! I am happy with these books!'

There is a breakthrough when a mother attends a meeting for a third time as she has children in three different year groups. In the first two meetings she expressed that she did not want her son taking part in these lessons, but in the third meeting she says she has changed her mind. She says that she was recently walking in the park with her eight-year-old son and when two men walked past them holding hands, she had felt panicked and did not know what to say but her son had said, 'It's OK, Mum, it's normal; they are just different.' The mother tells us she now understands what we are trying to do in school and that she supports us.

The vast majority of parents, once they have seen the books, leave saying they wish they had come earlier rather than worry because the books are not as they imagined they would be. My conclusion is that meetings are crucial to parent acceptance of the work and, consequently, the success of the work in school.

June: coffee meeting with Somali mothers

The school holds a coffee afternoon once a week with a group of Somali mothers. Following the parent meetings earlier in the year, a member of this group asked me to visit the group and explain about LGBT people and the work we are doing in school. The meeting went very well and demonstrates how far we have come in the last year; there was not one negative response and many talked calmly about living in the UK and wanting to show that they accept difference and diversity including gay people. Mothers talked about their children growing up and going to college and/or university where they may meet gay people and that they need to know that there are different people. One mother said she was worried that Year 2 was too young but another replied that children are already aware of gay and lesbian people – it's all around them on television and in the outside community – and the school needs to be talking about it so that children get the right messages.

June: One year on

The texts we are using in school have become part of the fabric of the school and no longer present challenges for teachers. I ask in Year 5 how the lesson on *My Princess Boy* went and the two teachers both said there had been no reaction from their classes because the children are used to talking about these issues now. One teacher remarks that the only time he gets a reaction is when he uses 'homosexual' or 'sexual orientation', sometimes getting a snigger because of the word 'sex' in these terms. When he uses 'gay' or 'lesbian', there is no reaction.

Since the parent meetings there has been only one complaint about the work we are doing, when a father approached the head teacher during our summer fête. However, the way we have involved parents over the past six months means there is really nothing more to say on the issue; parents had their opportunity to raise concerns at the year group meetings and there is no need to hold another round. From now on, in the first term of each academic year we will invite parents – again a year group at a time – to see the books we are using for this resource but I expect there to be less and less fear over the project the further down the line we go, and fewer and fewer attendees.

In May 2015, when I used the photo of the equality demonstration following the Irish equal marriage referendum, I did wonder whether there would be a response from parents, but there was none. I feel that now we have met with all parents who had concerns and shown them exactly what we are doing that the vast majority of parents are happy and supportive.

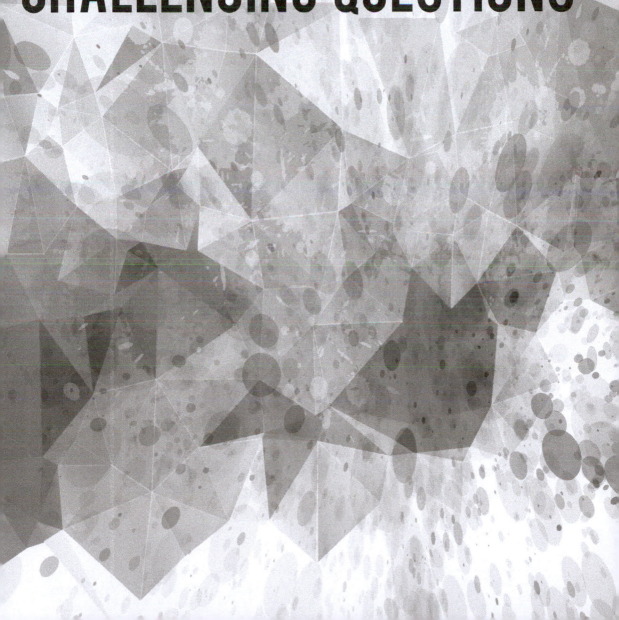

Chapter Five

SIMPLE ANSWERS TO CHALLENGING QUESTIONS

Simple answers to challenging questions

The following are all questions I have been asked by parents over the last five years. As I have never been asked about challenging racism or disability awareness or gender equality, all of these questions relate to challenging homophobia.

How do I explain what 'gay' means to my child?

'Gay' is when a man loves a man. 'Lesbian' is when two women love each other. 'Bi-sexual' is when a person can love both men and women. 'Transgender' is when a person feels different from the body they were born into; we were all assigned a gender at birth and sometimes when we get a bit older we may feel differently about that. Some people say there are 'boy things' and some say there are 'girl things', but we say that this is not the case and boys and girls can do the same sorts of things if they want. Some of us will live as a different gender from the one other people chose for us; others may like to do things that some people think are 'just for boys' or 'just for girls'.

But brothers love brothers and sisters love sisters and fathers love sons – does that make them gay?

Where two brothers love each other, it does not mean that they are gay. This is a different kind of love. We may love our mum but we don't want to marry our mum! Some people grow up and fall in love with a person of a different gender and some people grow up and fall in love with a person of the same gender, and sometimes these people may want to get married.

What do I say when my son comes home and asks, 'How can two men love each other?'

You say people are all different. Some men do love other men, and in the UK two men can get married in the same way that a man and a woman can get married or two women can get married.

What do I say when my son comes home and asks, 'How can two men have a baby?'

Lots of people have children in lots of different ways, like fostering, adoption or step-families. Some people change when they get older and families can change, too. These are all families; they look after one another and love one another so they are the same in many ways, regardless of how the children arrived.

Some families have a mum and a dad. Some families have a mum and a mum. Some families have two daddies. Some families have one mum or one dad or one gran or one grandad. Some children have two mums because one is a step-mum. All families are different and that's OK. The important thing to remember is that all families are welcome in our school.

Are primary children too young to be taught about gay or lesbian people?

Some children grow up in families with gay or lesbian people. We can't be saying to a child who has two dads, 'You can't talk about your family!' We want all of our children to know that their family is normal and accepted in school.

Are you teaching gay lessons?

We are teaching about equality. Our school ethos says that everyone is welcome and there are no outsiders. This means that if someone is black, they are welcome in school; if someone uses a wheelchair, they are welcome in school; and if someone is gay, they are welcome in school.

But no children are gay here, why does it need to be mentioned?

Some of our children may turn out to be gay or know gay people and they need to know that it's OK. We don't want any child in our school – gay or straight – to grow up thinking that there is something wrong with them. Also, some of our families may have gay people in them. All of our families are welcome here.

Can I remove my child from these lessons?

No. The law says you can remove your child from RE or sex education lessons but this is a lesson celebrating diversity. The lessons are not one-off sessions; the ethos is all around the school. It is not possible to shield children from our school ethos.

But my religion says that gay is wrong

We understand that and we respect all faiths here. We understand that this presents a tension for you. We are teaching children about the world around them and that there are gay and lesbian people in the world. We are preparing children for life in Britain where society is diverse and they are going to meet different people as they grow up. As they grow up, they can make up their own minds about what they believe to be right and wrong; we are simply giving them a rounded view of life.

You are going to make my child gay!

No, we are teaching your child not to be afraid of difference, and to celebrate difference. Reading a book cannot make a child gay. Visiting a farm does not make a child into a farmer. Visiting a different place of worship does not convert the child. Reading a book with gay characters in it does not make your child gay.

Do you have gay teachers on the staff?

I have no idea! We could have gay members on the staff and if we do they are very welcome at our school. Of course, someone's sexual orientation has nothing to do with their job.

Or:

Yes, we do! But that's irrelevant. Some of our teachers wear glasses and some of our teachers have brown eyes. One of our staff can wiggle his ears and I do believe one is left-handed … shall I go on?

You are confusing my child because at home they are learning that being gay is wrong but at school you are telling them that being gay is OK.

UK law says that gay people can get married and bring up children. We are teaching children that all families are different and your child is going to meet other children as they grow up who live in different families. It's important that children hear about people who are different. When they grow up, they can make up their own minds about what is right and wrong.

Chapter Six

COMING OUT IN PRIMARY SCHOOLS

Coming out in primary schools

There is an argument that gay and lesbian teachers should be out at school to children: after all, what better way is there to challenge homophobia than to be able to present as a gay role model? Often it does not occur to children that someone they know may be gay; gay people are an abstract concept – they exist somewhere, elsewhere!

However, I live in the real world and it's not always as easy as that. I have been out to children and parents in two schools. In the first the experience was extremely positive but in the second the experience was very damaging both to me and to any child watching who may end up identifying as gay. The law protects gay people in the workplace, but the law cannot protect that person from emotional fall-out following complaints from parents.

I would support and encourage any teacher who feels that they are ready to come out at school, and I would say to every school that they should be encouraging LGBT staff to be open about who they are in the same way that straight teachers are, without thinking. However, I would also recommend that schools prepare the ground before staff come out by demonstrating commitment to equality for all.

It is the school's responsibility to ensure that teachers are safe and the environment is one where diverse sexual orientation is accepted. Taking on schemes of work like this one will help to achieve that. I am convinced that in 20 years' time this book will be redundant because we will not be having these conversations, but in 2016 we cannot afford to be naïve.

How to come out at school

Over the years I have been asked by children if I am gay when I haven't been ready to come out. The answer I have given has been, 'Well I could be, couldn't I? There are thousands of gay people living in _____ [insert city].'

In a lesson on *And Tango Makes Three* a few years ago, a Year 5 boy asked me in front of the class if I was gay, and I replied, 'Am I gay? You're asking me to come out? But are gay people accepted in this school?'

There was a general 'Noooo!' in response.

I went on, 'Well, in that case I'm not going to tell you. If I thought this was a safe place to be gay – if I thought there would be no teasing or no laughing – then I would tell you, but I'm not sure. Your job is to convince me that this school is a safe place for gay people. Then I will tell you if I am gay or not.'

I have used this response many times. Even when children argue that the school is a safe place, I have quoted a homophobic comment recorded in a homophobic incident book: 'When there is no more homophobic name calling, then a person might choose to tell you that they are gay. But you have to make the school safe first.'

It's also good for children to realise that asking someone if they are gay is not really appropriate. A gay person will choose to tell you they are gay when they are ready, and that is usually when they trust you and your reaction. If you want a gay person to come out to you, then you have to show them in your behaviour that you are supportive.

It may be useful to explain the method I used to come out in both schools. I should say that I have always told colleagues that I am gay from the first day of entering a school. Again, this is a choice, but I have never been concerned about colleagues knowing.

In 2006 I had a civil partnership, and I thought that if ever there was a time to come out, then this was it. I imagined not telling my class that I was getting married and it seemed wrong. I have seen many schools mention straight people getting married in assemblies; often teachers change their name on getting married, which acts as a stimulus for the conversation. (Similarly, many teachers have photographs of loved ones and children on their desks; this is fine but it needs to be equal for gay people.)

I led a circle time in Year 5 and read *Dougal's Deep Sea Diary* by Simon Battram (2005). In the book, the character Dougal loves deep-sea diving but tells none of his work colleagues. At the end, he disappears to the beach never to return and the last page shows the bus to work with his empty seat. I said, 'Do you think it's a shame that Dougal never told his friends at work about his hobby? Why didn't he tell them? Now he's gone and they never knew that secret! Perhaps someone else at work also loves diving and they never knew!'

I asked the children how much we knew about one another in our class. I said, 'We've been together all year and some people you might have known since Reception but are there still things you don't know about the person sitting next to you? Play the Truth and Lies game: everyone gives three statements about themselves to the group but two are lies. Can you work out which statement is true?'

When it was my turn I said, 'I have four sisters. I was born in New Zealand. I'm getting married on Saturday.'

One of the children asked in front of the class, 'Are you getting married?'
'Yes,' I replied. 'To my partner, David.'

Then we continued the game. There was no big reaction.

I have discovered having done this a few times that children by and large don't care if someone is gay. Or at least they follow the reaction that is modelled to them by adults around them. I mentioned to the staff in the staffroom over lunch that I was going to reveal that I was getting married so that no one was shocked or flustered if a child asked them about it afterwards. I asked teachers to respond to questions if they came up from children with honesty, and I was relieved I had mentioned it because almost every teacher within 24 hours had a child ask them if it was true that Mr Moffat was gay, and they all replied, 'Yes … now get on with your work.'

I came out in my second school in 2013, four years after joining the team. Year 6 had done a lesson based on the book *King and King* and some children had made a poster with a title 'Gay is OK' and comments like, 'It doesn't matter if you are gay' and 'No outsiders here' which I decided to hold up in an assembly I was leading.

I asked the Year 6 children to explain what the book was about and then thanked them for doing the poster. I then said, 'It's a great example of what we say about no outsiders. In our school is it OK to be Muslim?'
The children replied, 'Yes!'

Ｒ Routledge

'Yes, Muslim is OK. Is it OK to be black?'

'Yes!'

'Yes, black is OK. In this school is it OK to be white?'

'Yes!'

'Yes, white is OK. In this school is it OK to wear glasses?'

This continued while I listed about 15 ways to be different. To each one the children cheered, 'Yes!'

I finished with, 'And in this school, is it OK to be gay?'

'Yes!'

'Yes, gay is OK. I'm gay and this poster makes me feel really welcome in this school, so thank you Year 6. Give them a clap!'

Again, there was no reaction whatsoever from the children and we carried on as normal, except now everyone knew a gay person!

Interestingly, once I had come out at that school, a child outed her mother as living with her girlfriend, and another child wrote in literacy about her tall, black gay brother. Here lies the reason it's so important for gay and lesbian staff to be out at school; those children only talked about their families once they knew that it was safe to do so. We need to be showing all children that their school is safe for LGBT people, and let us not forget that some of those children will turn out to be LGBT, too.

In 2015, in my current school, we managed to get the former rugby player Gareth Thomas to visit for an afternoon and I asked him if he would come out in an assembly at the end of the day, to which he agreed.

I read a book in this assembly called *World Team* by Tim Vyner (2002), which is about children all over the world playing football. At the end I said that this book was a good example of 'No outsiders in our school' because all of the children in the story were different yet they all liked football, and of course they would all be welcome at our school. I said, 'I wonder in what ways are we different to one another?'

Ⓡ Routledge
Taylor & Francis Group

I had primed the staff to give me ways in which they were different and also told Gareth what I wanted him to say. The first teacher put up their hand and said they were a mum and I said, 'Great – mums are welcome at Parkfield School!' The second teacher put up their hand and said they were black, and I said, 'Great – black people are welcome at our school!' We carried on with people outing themselves as being from Northern Ireland, as being of mixed race, as being a grandma and as being from Pakistan. Then Gareth put up his hand and said he was from Wales so I said, 'Great – people from Wales are welcome at Parkfield School.' Then he said that there was another thing: he was gay. I was then able to say, 'Great – gay people are welcome at our school!' There was one audible gasp from a child in Year 6 but otherwise there was no reaction at all, which was quite nice because it demonstrated to the shocked child that he was alone in his reaction; his homophobia made him the outsider. For everyone else this was not newsworthy.

At the time of writing, I am not yet out to the children at my school but I have no doubt I will be soon. In my first school I waited six years and in my second school four years. I've been here just a year so far so perhaps in the next 12 months I will be ready. Following the success of the work on 'No outsiders' that we have been doing for the last 12 months, I feel more confident than ever that our path is prepared and it is the right thing to do.

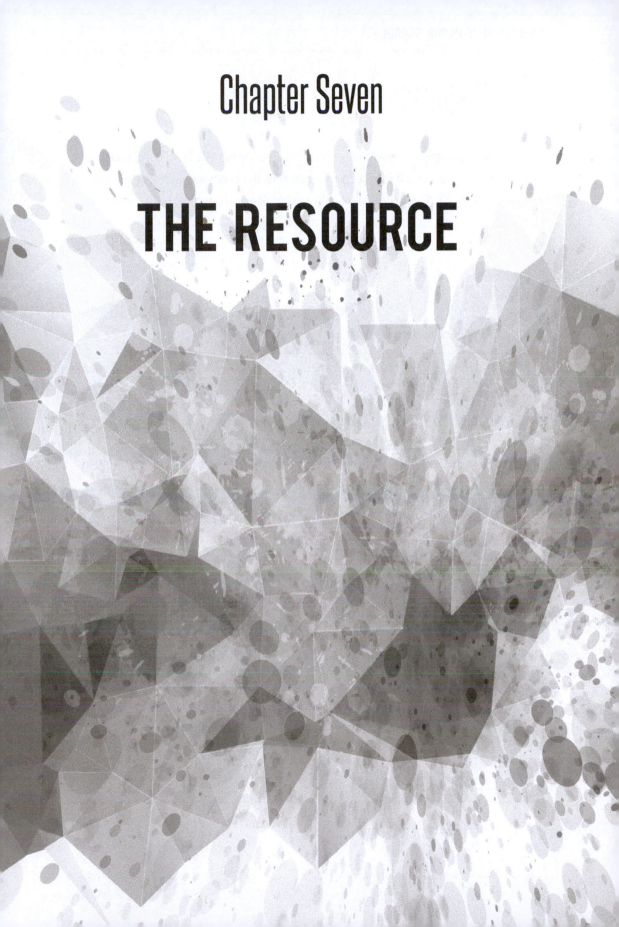

Chapter Seven

THE RESOURCE

The resource

Rather than separating the characteristics of the Equality Act 2010 and using books to specifically teach about religion, gender or disability, the books in this resource focus on diversity as a whole. There are some books to specifically support the LGBT strand, but otherwise the books can be used to celebrate diversity in all its forms. The full list of books recommended here – broken down by the year groups they are appropriate for – is given in Table 7.1 and each of Tables 7.2 to 7.37 gives the details of how to make use of one of the texts (in the order given in Table 7.1).

Table 7.1: Book list for Reception–Year 6

EYFS	You Choose (by Nick Sharratt and Pippa Goodheart)	Red Rockets and Rainbow Jelly (by Sue Heap and Nick Sharratt)	Blue Chameleon (by Emily Gravett)	The Family Book (by Todd Parr)	Mommy Mama and Me (by Leslea Newman and Carol Thompson)
Year 1	Elmer (by David Mckee)	Ten Little Pirates (by Mike Brownlow and Simon Rickerty)	My Grandpa is Amazing (by Nick Butterworth)	Max the Champion (by Sean Stockdale, Alexandra Strick and Ros Asquith)	My World, Your World (by Melanie Walsh)
Year 2	The Great Big Book of Families (by Mary Hoffman and Ros Asquith)	The First Slodge (by Jeanne Willis)	The Odd Egg (by Emily Gravett)	Just Because (by Rebecca Elliot)	Blown Away (by Rob Biddulph)
Year 3	Oliver (by Birgitta Sif)	This Is Our House (by Michael Rosen)	Two Monsters (by David McKee)	The Hueys in the New Jumper (by Oliver Jeffers)	Beegu (by Alexis Deacon)
Year 4	Dogs Don't Do Ballet (by Anna Kemp and Sarah Ogilvie)	King and King (by Linda de Hann and Stern Nijland)	The Way Back Home (by Oliver Jeffers)	The Flower (by John Light)	Red: A Crayon's Story (by Michael Hall)

Routledge Taylor & Francis Group

Year 5	Where the Poppies Now Grow (by Hilary Robinson and Martin Impey)	Rose Blanche (by Ian McEwan and Roberto Innocenti)	How to Heal a Broken Wing (by Bob Graham)	The Artist Who Painted a Blue Horse (by Eric Carle)	And Tango Makes Three (by Justin Richardson and Peter Parnell)
Year 6	My Princess Boy (by Cheryl Kilodavis and Suzanne DeSimone)	The Whisperer (by Nick Butterworth)	The Island (by Armin Greder)	Love You Forever (by Robert Munsch)	Dreams of Freedom (by Amnesty International)

Table 7.2: EYFS: LI: To say what I think

Text: *You Choose* (by Nick Sharratt and Pippa Goodheart)
Learning intention: To say what I think
Success criteria. I can tell you the things I like and I can make my own mind up and I can ask others what they think.
Starter. Show the children the front cover of the book. Ask them what they think 'You choose' means. Ask them what they think the book is going to be about.
Main. Read *You Choose*. During the first reading, do not ask the children for their opinions.
Role play. Say that you are going to read the text again but this time you want to know which objects the children would choose. Explain that you are going to stop at each page on this reading and ask children for their opinion. Use name cards to select children at random. Read the first page and then ask a child to choose their favourite image on the page. Then take the next name card, give it to the named child and say, 'You choose.' Continue through the book until everyone has had a go at selecting an image.
Activity. Give the children different images of random objects and foods. The children sort the images and then stick them in their assessment book under the headings 'I like' and 'I don't like'.
Plenary. Say, 'We all had a turn choosing in the game. That was fair. Why do you think it was important that everyone got a turn to choose? How would you have felt if you had missed your turn? Lots of us chose different things – does that matter? Is it OK to like different things? That is what I like about this class; even though we are all different and like different things, we like one another and we all get a chance to talk. What a great class this is!'
Assessment for Learning (AFL) questions. What have we learned today? What did I choose today? What did another child choose today?

Table 7.3: EYFS: LI: To understand that it's OK to like different things

Text: *Red Rockets and Rainbow Jelly* (by Sue Heap and Nick Sharratt)
Learning intention: To understand that it's OK to like different things
Success criteria. I know my friends can like different things to me, and I know that we can still be friends.
Starter. Put up images of different fruit on the board: apples, bananas and oranges. In pairs, the children discuss their favourite of these. Ask the children if, within the pairs, there was any disagreement as to what was the preferred fruit.
Main. Discuss the learning intention. Read the text from start to finish. Ask the children to talk in pairs to recall things that Nick liked and things that Sue liked. Children feed back to the class as a whole. Reinforce: 'What a lot of different things! Were Nick and Sue friends? So even though they liked different things, did they still like each other?'
Role play. Ask the children in pairs to think of one thing that they both like. For example, maybe they both like swings or perhaps they both like apples. Each pair feeds back to the class. Now double-up the pairs so that the children are in groups of four and repeat the Activity. Double the group again and repeat the exercise. Repeat again in even larger groups and then, finally, do the task as a whole class. As a whole class the teacher should lead the discussion: 'Now, look at us: we are all different. There are children here with long hair and children with short hair. There are children with different colour skins and children with different eye colours, and we are all different shapes and sizes. I wonder, even though we are all different, can we find one thing we all like?' Encourage the children to give suggestions and then ask others to agree or disagree with these until you reach a consensus. At the end, reinforce how brilliant it is that we are all different yet we all like X. (If children nominate people for what is liked, encourage a discussion about objects instead.)
Activity. Draw and label different children in the class. Ask them what they like. Write it under the picture; for example, 'Ben likes jelly.' Children should also draw themselves and write a sentence about what they like. In the middle of the page write, 'We are all friends.'
Plenary. Say, 'Today, we found things that we all liked, but there are lots of ways in which we are different, too.' In pairs, children discover differences in what they like; for example, Daniel may like chocolate and Tajein may like peas. Daniel feeds back, 'I like chocolate, Tajein likes peas and we are still friends.' Tajein then says, 'I like peas, Daniel likes chocolate and we are still friends.'
AFL questions. What would life be like if we all liked the same things? Is it OK to be different?

R Routledge Taylor & Francis Group

Table 7.4: EYFS: LI: To make friends with someone different

Text: *Blue Chameleon* (by Emily Gravett)
Learning intention: To make friends with someone different
Success criteria. I know that everyone is different in my class, and I can make friends with anyone.
Starter. Show an image on the board of two friends. Ask, 'What is the same about them? What is different?'
Main. Read the text from start to finish. Say, 'Why does Blue Chameleon feel lonely at the beginning? Why does he say hello to all of the different objects and animals? How does he feel when everyone ignores him? Why does he give up near the end? What changes to make him happy? How does he feel at the end when the other chameleon says hi?'
Role play. Say, 'Let's all be chameleons.' Explain that the members of the class are going to stand in a circle and when you ring a bell or bang on a tambourine, you want children to come to the middle of the circle, find a new friend and say, 'Hello.' (If there is an odd number of children in the class then ask for one child each game to help you in order to ensure that no one is left out by pairing up children.) Children go back into the circle with their new friend. Repeat. On each occasion children must find a different 'friend'. Repeat until ten new friends have been found.
Activity. Give children blank outlines of two chameleons to colour. The resulting chameleons should each be a different colour. Give each chameleon a speech bubble so that children can write a greeting in each bubble.
Plenary. Look at the two chameleons at the end. Say, 'Are they the same colour? No! Are they still friends? Of course! Can you be friends with someone who is different from you? Of course you can!'
AFL question. What have you learned today about being different from your friend but still being friends?

Table 7.5: EYFS: LI: To understand that all families are different

Text: *The Family Book* (by Todd Parr)
Learning intention: To understand that all families are different
Success criteria. I know who is in my family. I know that all families are different.
Starter. Put the word 'family' on the board. Ask the children, 'What is a family?'
Main. Read the text from start to finish. Ask the children to talk in pairs to recall the different families mentioned in the book and to then feed back to the class. Ask the children, 'Were there any families in the book that were like your family?' Focus on the pages 'All families like to hug each other'. Ask, 'Why?'
Role play. Show the children a baby doll and explain that this baby needs a family. Say, 'Who will look after it? What do babies need? They need hugs, care and love.' Ask for a volunteer to look after the baby and hand the doll over to them. Praise the child for holding the baby carefully and talking softly in order to keep the baby calm. Ask the child who they want in their family. The child then chooses any number of children to be in their family and they pass the baby doll around, showing they can all care for it. Praise the 'family', and then ask for a new volunteer to look after the baby and choose a new family. Continue until everyone who wants a turn being in a family has had one. Highlight the fact that the families are all different as they are being chosen and reinforce that all families are different and that's OK.
Activity. Children draw their family and label the members.
Plenary. Say, 'Today, we talked about different families. Are all the families in our class the same? What different families do we have? One mum? One dad? Mum and dad? Two mums? Two dads? One nan? Two nans? What have we learned today? All families are different and that's OK.'
AFL questions. What is a family? What have you learned about families being different but that being OK?

Table 7.6: EYFS: LI: To celebrate my family

Text: *Mommy Mama and Me* (by Leslea Newman and Carol Thompson)
Learning intention: To celebrate my family
Success criteria. I know the people in my family are special, and I can tell you who loves me.
Starter. Go around the circle with children saying what is their favourite thing to do at home.
Main. Read *Mommy Mama and Me* from start to finish. Say, 'Who is the book about? What do they like doing together? Is there anything in the book you like doing with other members of your family? Which activities are your favourite?'
Role play. Make a list with the children of the activities in the book. Consider whether anyone can act out any of the activities. Stand in a circle and ask for a volunteer to act out one of the activities. Once other children recognise the activity, they should join in until everyone is role playing the activity. Exclaim, 'What fun it is when we join in together!'
Activity. Children draw and record a sentence for activities they like doing at home with someone in their family.
Plenary. Look at the child's facial expression on each page. Ask, 'How are they feeling? How do we know? Why do you think the child feels happy? [It is because Mommy and Mama love the child.] Who loves you in your family?'
AFL questions. What is your family good at?   Who loves you in your family?

Table 7.7: Year 1: LI: To like the way I am

Text: *Elmer* (by David McKee)
Learning intention: To like the way I am
Success criteria. I know the ways in which we are different and I know how to make my class welcoming.
Starter. Prepare a collage on the interactive whiteboard of children from different ethnic and cultural origins. Include images of children in different clothing. Children should identify differences in appearance between the children shown.
Main. Read *Elmer* from start to finish. When Elmer changes, ask the children why they believe he is doing that and what they think will happen next. Talk about Elmer being different in the story. Say, 'Did he like being different at the start? How does he try to fit in? Should Elmer try to change the colour of his skin?'
Role play. Sit the children in a circle and place a large cut-out figure of Elmer in the middle of the group. Place a bowl of different coloured squares next to the cut-out. Explain that the aim will be to make a model of Elmer in order to celebrate his difference and show him that if he came to our class, he would be welcome. Say, 'We are going to celebrate the different colours that make Elmer who he is. He needs to know that it is OK to be different.' Ask the children to choose a coloured square and glue it on to Elmer. When he is complete, hold him up and start a round of applause. Say, 'Isn't he beautiful!'
Activity. Give children images representing three key events from the story: (1) the picture where the elephants are asleep and Elmer is thinking, (2) the picture where he covers himself in berries and (3) the picture where the berries are washed off. The children should describe how Elmer is feeling at each of the different sections of the story.
Plenary. Say, 'Why did Elmer want to fit in? If Elmer was in our class, what would we do and say to him to make sure he didn't feel the way he felt?' Go around the circle asking children to say things that would help Elmer to like the way he is. Put Elmer on the wall so the children understand that if he ever did come to the school, he would know that he is welcome and that people like him the way he is.
AFL questions. What does it feel like to be different? Why do we like different people in our school?

Table 7.8: Year 1: LI: To play with boys and girls

Text: *Ten Little Pirates* (by Mike Brownlow and Simon Rickerty)
Learning intention: To play with boys and girls
Success criteria: I know boys play exciting games, and I know girls can play exciting games, and I know boys and girls can play together.
Starter. Say, 'With a partner identify two exciting games you like to play. Why do you like them? Who plays the game with you?'
Main. Read *Ten Little Pirates* from start to finish. Say, 'What exciting things do the pirates do? Why are the numbers counting down? What happens at the end? Are any pirates left out of the games and activities? Why not?' [The pirates make sure that no one is left out.]
Role play. Role play the story at the front of the class with ten children playing the role of pirates and other children role playing the obstacles (shark, hurricane, and so on). Make sure there is a mix of boys and girls in the pirate group. You may want to make the point that girls can be pirates, too, and, furthermore, that some boys may not want to be a pirate and that's OK.
Activity. Say, 'We all play with one another in our class; boys and girls can play every game in school.' Children choose one of the pirate activities from the book and record boys and girls in the class carrying it out. Label the children you choose to draw.
Plenary. Say, 'Are some games only for boys and some games only for girls? No! In our school everyone can play any game they wish! It's not obvious in the book whether the pirates are boys or girls, which is great for the lesson because everyone joins in together.' Make a list of games that boys and girls can play together in the school. End by saying, 'That's what I like about our class – you all make sure that no one is left out and everyone joins in if they want to.'
AFL questions. Say, 'Are some games only for boys?' Establish that this is not so. Say, 'Are some games only for girls?' Establish that this is not so. Say, 'What do we say in our school about boys and girls playing?' Establish that this is that boys and girls can play together and play the same things if they want to.

Table 7.9: Year 1: LI: To recognise that people are different ages

Text: *My Grandpa Is Amazing* (by Nick Butterworth)
Learning intention: To recognise that people are different ages
Success criteria. I know that we all grow up, and I can tell you good things about being older.
Starter. Show an image on the board of a large family photograph with children, parents and grandparents. The children should identify how the people in the photograph are likely to be related to one another.
Main. Read *My Grandpa is Amazing*. Say, 'What is the best thing about Grandpa in the book?' Children discuss in pairs and then feed back. Say, 'Grandpa seems to be always smiling. Why do you think that is? How old do you think Grandpa may be? Has Grandpa always been this age? How has he got to be this age? Is Grandpa happy? How do you know?'
Role play. The aim is to demonstrate to the children that people should not be discriminated against because of age, so to show a grandparent working is a great example. If there is a member of staff at school who is a grandparent, ask them to visit the class, show photos of their grandchildren and talk about their family. Children should plan questions to ask. They could also show *My Grandpa Is Amazing* and ask if the grandparent visiting is similar to Grandpa. If any of the children's grandparents are working or have interesting or active hobbies to talk about, you could lead a discussion about these instead.
Activity. Children draw a picture of Grandpa from the story and label around the image with all of the things that he is good at.
Plenary. Say, 'Are there activities that Grandpa does in the book that we can't do? When will we be able to do those things? Why is growing older a good thing?'
AFL questions. What have you learned today? What will you be able to do when you are older?

Routledge Taylor & Francis Group

Table 7.10: Year 1: LI: To understand that our bodies work in different ways

Text: *Max the Champion* (by Sean Stockdale, Alexandra Strick and Ros Asquith)
Learning intention: To understand that our bodies work in different ways
Success criteria. I know that everyone is different and I know that you can't always see difference.
Starter. Show the children the front cover of the book. In pairs, the children predict what they think will happen in the story or what they think Max will be like.
Main. Read and discuss *Max the Champion*. Say, 'What kind of person is Max? Is Max shy or confident? How do you know? Does Max ever speak in the story? I wonder why not? Does he have friends? Does he look happy? Why do you think Max is happy?' Instruct the children to look at the page where Max shows his art pictures. Say, 'Is there anything different about Max? What is he using to help him breathe?' Instruct the children to look at the same page again. Say, 'Is there anything else different about Max? Max is wearing a hearing aid. What is a hearing aid? How does it help Max? Has anyone in the class got any experiences of inhalers or hearing aids that they could share?' Discuss how inhalers and hearing aids help any child who uses them.
Role play. Role play the story with children acting out as a group all the things that Max does. Start with Max waking up and running (on the spot) downstairs and then continue to him eating breakfast, biking to school, and so on. End with everyone sleeping.
Activity. Draw Max with his hearing aid or his inhaler doing the things he likes doing most. Record 'Max is a champion at . . .'
Plenary. Say, 'Does the hearing aid or the inhaler stop Max doing the things he loves? Is Max happy and confident? Do the other children like Max? Of course they do! It's like in our class when someone has different needs and we help them and we all get along! What a fantastic place our school is – everyone helps one another and nobody is left out.'
AFL questions. What have we learned today? What have we learned about one way in which our bodies work differently?

Ⓡ Routledge
Taylor & Francis Group

Table 7.11: Year 1: LI: To understand that we share the world with lots of people

Text: *My World, Your World* (by Melanie Walsh)
Learning intention: To understand that we share the world with lots of people
Success criteria. I know I live in the world and I know that the world is full of different people.
Starter. Stand in a circle in order to play 'The Sun Shines On'. Explain that everyone wearing black shoes swaps places when you say, 'The sun shines on everyone who has black shoes.' Next say, 'The sun shines on everyone who has brown eyes.' Everyone with brown eyes swaps places. Repeat for having blue eyes, liking bananas, liking ice cream, and so on.
Main. Read *My World, Your World* from start to finish. Ask, 'Are there any children in the class who do the same things as the children in the book?'
Role play. Play 'The Sun Shines On' again using the text. Explain that anyone wearing a sari moves when you say, 'The sun shines on everyone who wears a sari to school.' Then say, 'The sun shines on everyone who wears a warm jacket and snow boots to school.' Then say, 'The sun shines on everyone who wears trainers to PE.' Then stop the game and ask, 'How are we different to Kavita? How are we the same as Kavita? How are we different to Jacob? How are we the same as Jacob?' Go through the book playing the game for each pair of children. If no one does the things that the characters share (for example, riding skateboards) then ask, 'Can the class think of anything else that they may share with the characters?' [For example, enjoying playing outside.]
Activity. Give the children an image of the world to stick in their books. Put up the image of the cover of the book on the whiteboard. Children write a sentence about people sharing the world or about different people living together in the world. Alternatively, they could copy the cover of the book. Children draw an image of two children with different skin colours or different clothes next to the world to show an understanding of diversity.
Plenary. Say, 'What is the world?' Hold up a globe. Ask, 'Where do we live? What other countries are there in the world? Has anyone been to another country?'
AFL questions. What have I learned today? In which country do I live? Who do I share the world with?

Table 7.12: Year 2: LI: To understand what diversity is

Text: *The Great Big Book of Families* (by Mary Hoffman and Ros Asquith)
Learning intention: To understand what diversity is
Success criteria. I understand what diversity means and I know how my school is diverse.
Starter. Say, 'What is diversity?' If children don't know, tell them that it means everyone being different. Children should come up with different people who are welcome at the school, and feed back to the class.
Main. Read *The Great Big Book of Families* from start to finish. At the end, ask the children how the book helps us to understand what diversity is. Ask, 'What examples of diversity are there in the book?'
Role play. Show the children cards with the following headings: transport, celebrations, jobs, families, homes, religions. Explain that we are going to play the diversity game. One child takes a card and reads it out, and then the child next to them thinks of an example of something that would fit into that category, and then the next child thinks of another example, and so on until the children run out of ideas. Put the score on the board – for example, three points if the children have suggested Eid, Christmas and Diwali for 'celebrations'. Ask, 'Can we beat our diversity score on the next card?' [For the families card, ask the children to think of different families in the book – mum and dad, dad and dad, mum and mum, one mum, one dad, and so on.]
Activity. Tell the children that it's great to live in the UK because we are so diverse. Give the children an outline map of the UK and tell them that around it they should record the ways in which we celebrate diversity – different religions, different families, different genders, and so on.
Plenary. Imagine if we lived in a place where everyone was the same and did the same things every day. Ask, 'What would it be like? Are lots of countries diverse? Why is diversity a good thing?'
AFL questions. What have I learned today? What does 'diversity' mean?

Table 7.13: Year 2: LI: To understand how we share the world

Text: *The First Slodge* (by Jeanne Willis)
Learning intention: To understand how we share the world
Success criteria. I know there are people who are different from me, and I know I can share the world with different people, and I know that I can get along with different people.
Starter. Show a globe. Ask, 'How many countries can you name?'
Main. Read the text from *The First Slodge*. Say, 'What does Slodge think when she first sees the world? Why does she think that? What changes? When the two Slodges first meet they look different. What do you think they feel inside? How do they become friends? What do they learn at the end of the story?'
Role play. Look at the page near the end. Say, 'The world didn't belong to anyone. It belonged to everyone. It was there to share. What are the Slodges doing in the picture? [They are sharing food.] Is anyone saying, "I'm a rabbit and rabbits don't share food with foxes!"? Is anyone saying, "I'm a bird and birds don't share with elephants!"?' Show the children a plate of food (holding biscuits or fruit pieces – enough for one each). Tell the children that they can all share the food but first they have to offer it to someone else and say how they are different; for example, a child may say, 'I have brown hair, you have blond hair, we can still share.' Continue until everyone has a biscuit or piece of fruit. Children should wait until everyone has some food before they eat.
Activity. Around an image of the globe the children should record people they share the world with. They could refer to *The Great Big Book of Families* for guidance.
Plenary. Say, 'What would happen if one group of people decided they did not want to share? When there was an earthquake in Nepal in 2015, what did people around the world do? Why? Why is it good to work with people who are different from us?'
AFL questions. What have I learned today? Who do I share the world with?

Table 7.14: Year 2: LI: To understand what makes someone feel proud

Text: *The Odd Egg* (by Emily Gravett)
Learning intention: To understand what makes someone feel proud
Success criteria. I know that things can go wrong, and I know that when things go wrong I can feel embarrassed and I can find a solution.
Starter. Show an image of a hen sitting on an egg. Say, 'What is happening in the picture? What will happen to the eggs if they are left with the hen?'
Main. Read and discuss *The Odd Egg*. Say, 'Why does this book have that title – what does "odd" mean? How do you think the birds feel when they have laid their eggs? [The birds feel proud.] Does the duck feel proud when he finds an egg? How do we know? [He thought that it was the most beautiful egg in the whole world.] Look at the ducks teasing him. How does he feel about it? How do the birds feel when their eggs hatch? Right before his egg hatches, how is the duck feeling? Do you think the duck feels proud or ashamed when a crocodile comes out?'
Role play. Act out the story using blankets to cover the children before they hatch. Read the story again and put some children in the middle of the circle with their 'eggs' (that is, their partners). As each egg hatches, have the child showing pride in their new baby and taking the baby to join the circle. Leave the duck and his egg until last and build up tension by knocking on the shell and saying, 'It's not coming out!' Get all the children to lean in expectantly while the egg begins to hatch and then count down from three before the croc bursts out and everyone screams. (Remind the child playing the croc that in the story the croc doesn't actually hurt or touch anyone.) End the role play by having the croc turn to the duck and say, 'Mama!' as they return to the circle. Give the children a round of applause.
Activity. The children should draw a picture of the croc bursting out from the egg with a speech bubble to show what the duck feels. (Examples of text for the speech bubble would include: 'I still love you even though you are different', 'I am proud of you' and 'It doesn't matter that you're not a duck'.)
Plenary. Say, 'Some people may say that the duck can't look after his baby because he is a croc. What would you say if you heard the other birds say, "That's not a real family"? Can it be a real family?' [Yes, it can – if the duck wants to look after a croc then he is allowed to. All families are different.]
AFL questions. What have you learned today? Why does the duck feel proud of his baby?

Table 7.15: Year 2: LI: To feel proud of being different

Text: *Just Because* (by Rebecca Elliot)
Learning intention: To feel proud of being different
Success criteria. I know that some bodies work in different ways, and I can find things that people are good at.
Starter. In pairs, children find two ways in which they are the same as each other and two ways in which they are different and then feed back.
Main. Read *Just Because* from start to finish. Say, 'What things can't Clemmie do? Does it matter why she can't do those things? What does her sister say when people ask why she can't do them? What does Clemmie use to get around? [She uses a wheelchair.] Why does she use one? [Possible answers are because her body works in a different way and a chair helps her move, or 'Just because!' – we are all different and that's just the way it is.]
Role play. Turn to the page where Clemmie makes sweet noises, pulls funny faces and wears silly hats. Say, 'If Clemmie visited us, what could we do to make her feel welcome? Let's make silly hats so that if Clemmie does ever come to visit the school, we can show her our hats and swap them – then she will feel welcome.'
Activity. Use the hat making in 'role play' as an art activity.
Plenary. Say, 'We all now have hats that we could share with Clemmie. What else could we do with Clemmie if she came to visit? Is there anything about our school that Clemmie would find difficult? What could we change so that she could join in?'
AFL questions. What have I learned today? What is it that both Clemmie and I like which means that we can be friends with each other?

Table 7.16: Year 2: LI: To be able to work with everyone in my class

Text: *Blown Away* (by Rob Biddulph)
Learning intention: To be able to work with everyone in my class
Success criteria. I know that everyone in my class is different and I can work with anyone, and I like working with different people.
Starter. Play the five-second swap game. Put a hoop in the middle of the circle and explain that a rule of the game is that there has to be three children in the hoop at all times. Count down from five to one with three children moving into the hoop as you do so. Count down from five to one again with three different children moving into the hoop. Continue until everyone has had a turn. Children are not allowed to just move round the circle three at a time, rather the three children need to be taken at random. If four children move into the hoop one must leave. This is a game to promote cooperation.
Main. Read the text from start to finish. Discuss the characters. How do they know one another? Are they the same animals or are they different? Does any character in the story ever say, 'No, I'm not helping you!'? Why not?
Role play. Role play the story. Ask a child to be a penguin and to hold on to an imaginary kite. The penguin should be 'blown around the circle' holding on to the kite as you read the book again, until Jeff and Flo hold the penguin's hand and are pulled along. Add more animals to the line and have them 'pulled' around the circle. (One child could be the kite.) You could add more animals to the story – joining on the end of the line – by asking children to suggest an animal they could be that wants to help. See if the whole class can join the line one by one. Have any children not involved (or you, if all of the children are in the line) blow them off the island as 'a gust of wind'. Have the children in the line get dropped off one by one, waving goodbye to their new friends as they go. At the end, everyone should be sitting back in the circle.
Activity. Pull random lolly sticks from a pot with names on to identify groups of five children. Send each group to a table to draw one another on a kite string. Each group should record their kite line and label the helping friends on their line.
Plenary. Some people may say that different animals can't be friends because they are different from each other – bears can't be friends with seals, and seals can't be friends with penguins. Say, 'What do we say in our school if people are different from one another? Can different people get along and help one another? Of course they can! We say that there are no outsiders in our school. What does that mean? [It means that no one is left out and that everyone is welcome.] Are there any outsiders in the story? What about the monkey who tags along without being noticed? He is a bit like an outsider because, as no one knows that he is there, no one talks to him. Do you think if the monkey had asked to come along, the animals would have let him? What should he have said to them? Why do you think he didn't say anything? How do we make sure no one feels like the monkey in our school? How do we make sure there are no outsiders?'
AFL questions. What have I learned today? How do I know that I can work with anyone in my class?

Table 7.17: Year 3: LI: To understand how difference can affect someone

Text: *Oliver* (by Birgitta Sif)
Learning intention: To understand how difference can affect someone
Success criteria. I know that we are all different in my class and I understand how difference can make people feel excluded.
Starter. In pairs, children come up with definitions for 'excluded' and 'included'.
Main. Read *Oliver* from start to finish. Study the images in the text as well as reading the words and ask the children to talk about the different feelings presented in the pictures. Say, 'Why do you think that Oliver plays by himself all the time? Is he happy? Look at the page where he is looking out of the window and talk about the emotions. What changes for Oliver? We don't know who spoke first, but who do you think spoke first and what do you think they said? Why does the final page say "The beginning" when it is the end of the book?'
Role play. Give everyone a slip of paper and ask them to write on it one way they think that they are different from everyone else. Then each person folds their paper tightly into a square. Show the children a jam jar (or some other container) and place it in the middle of the circle. Tell everyone that this is 'our difference jar'. Ask children, one at a time, to come to the centre of the circle and place their particular 'difference' in the difference jar. As they are doing it they should say, 'I am different' but not reveal how. Once everyone has placed their paper in the jar, shake it up and seal it. It can then be displayed as a reminder of differences existing in the classroom. Refer to it in the future if there is any bullying about someone being different.
Activity. With a partner, each child draws themselves and their partner in both of their books. Label with their names and write, 'I am different and so are you.'
Plenary. Say, 'We are all different in our class but, unlike Oliver, we make sure that there are no outsiders and no one is left out. How do we do that? If Oliver came to our school, what would you say to make him feel welcome?'
AFL questions. What have I learned today? What reasons can I give for it being OK to be different?

Table 7.18: Year 3: LI: To understand what 'discrimination' means

Text: *This Is Our House* (by Michael Rosen)
Learning intention: To understand what 'discrimination' means
Success criteria. I know how someone can feel like an outsider, and I know how to make sure that there are no outsiders in my school.
Starter. Show an image of children on a playground. Identify children in the picture who are included and children in the picture who are excluded. Ask, 'How can you tell?'
Main. Read *This Is Our House* from start to finish. Say, 'What are the reasons that George gives for not allowing people in to his house? What does "discrimination" mean? How is George showing discrimination? What does the term "outsider" mean? Who is made to feel like an outsider in the story? How does George change at the end of the story?'
Role play. Ask the children to write on a label one thing about them – such as what they like doing, their faith or their ethnicity. When all of the children are wearing their labels, tell them that you are going to play the part of George in the story. Explain that this is going to be very hard because George says things that you would never say. Wear a hat when you are speaking as George so that when you take off the hat you are back as yourself and the discriminatory things that George says are gone along with the hat.   Show the children a mat at the front of the class and explain that this is your house. Now ask children one at a time to come to your house and ask to come in. Tell each child they cannot come in because of their label; for example, you may say, 'There are no Christians in my house' or, 'There are no black people in my house' or, 'People who like football are not welcome in my house'. There will be a reaction from the children but remind them that this is what George says. After four or five children have tried to enter the house, take off the hat and tell the children how hard that was for you because those lines were things you have never said and that have no place in our school. Throw the hat away and tell the children that you never want to have to wear it again.   Ask the same children who tried to come into the house to come back and ask again. This time say, for example, 'Of course! Christian people are welcome in my house.'   At the end, exclaim how much better you feel now that it is clear that everyone is welcome and now that no one faces discrimination.
Activity. Children design a poster with the title 'This is our school!'. Children demonstrate on the poster that everyone is welcome in the school and there are no outsiders.
Plenary. Ask, 'What can we learn from this book? How can we make sure that no one feels like an outsider in our school?'
AFL questions. What have I learned today?   What do I understand 'discrimination' to mean?

Ⓡ Routledge
Taylor & Francis Group

Table 7.19: Year 3: LI: To find a solution to a problem

Text: *Two Monsters* (by David McKee)
Learning intention: To find a solution to a problem
Success criteria. I understand where some problems come from and I can find a solution to a problem.
Starter. Show images of children from around the world, living in different situations. Ask, 'Are we the same as these children or different?' List the similarities.
Main. Read *Two Monsters*. Say, 'How does the argument start? Why do the monsters think the other is wrong? Which is the first to make the wrong choice? The second monster could have responded differently – how? The monsters call each other many different names – how does name-calling affect the situation? How does the argument end? What do the monsters realise? How did they become friends at the end?' Explain that the monsters fought because they didn't communicate; they thought that the other was different and didn't listen to each other. Say, 'Do we listen to one another in our class? Do we know about one another?'
Role play. Divide the class into two. Place at least ten chairs across the middle of the room. Explain that the chairs are like the mountain. Say, 'Right now the chairs divide the class and we can't work together. Our job is to remove the chairs. The monsters used rocks to smash the mountain and we are going to use our knowledge of one another to remove the mountain.' Ask the children to think about something they share with another child on the other side of the mountain and to say this out loud. For example, a child might say, 'Essa and I are both good at maths.' For every positive statement, a chair is removed until they have all gone and you can say that the 'mountain' has been demolished. As the last chair is removed, the two groups of children cheer and approach each other to shake hands. All shout, 'We did it!'
Activity. The children should draw a picture showing themselves on one side of the page and another child in their class on the other and label with their names. In the middle of the page, in between the images, they should list the ways in which they are similar to the other child.
Plenary. Say, 'Should we show respect to different faiths and communities? Why? Why is showing respect to others important? Are the monsters showing respect to one another in the story? How did we show respect in our role play?'
AFL questions. What have I learned today? What do I know about how to sort out problems?

Table 7.20: Year 3: LI: Use strategies to help someone who feels different

Text: *The Hueys in the New Jumper* (by Oliver Jeffers)
Learning intention: Use strategies to help someone who feels different
Success criteria. I know why it's hard to be different and I know how to help someone to be strong.
Starter. Show the children the image at the start of the story where all of the Hueys are the same. Say 'What would it feel like if you lived there but thought that things should be different? What would stop you from speaking out?'
Main. Read *The Hueys in the New Jumper* from start to finish. Children discuss, in talk partners, how to come up with a description of what the story is about. Each pair should then feed back, saying, 'The new jumper is about …' Discuss what happens to Rupert throughout the story. Ask, 'Does he feel happy throughout the whole story? Why not?' Ask, 'What does the expression "stood out like a sore thumb" mean?'
Role play. Role play the section of the story where Rupert first wears a new jumper. Have a group of three, one child playing the part of Rupert, one child telling him to take off his jumper and one child playing the role of Gillespie, supporting Rupert. Give Rupert a new jumper to wear. Say, 'Is it easy to show empathy? How would Rupert have felt if Gillespie hadn't been around? What was the impact on Rupert of Gillespie showing empathy and on the rest of the Hueys?' Alternatively, you wear a new jumper and ask children first to role play the Hueys being shocked – asking the children to recognise how this behaviour makes you feel – and then ask children to role play what Gillespie does and discuss the different ways that makes you feel.
Activity. Ask children to focus on four different events in the story: one where Rupert is first wearing his jumper; one where the Hueys are pointing at him in horror; one where Gillespie knits a matching jumper; and one where lots of Hueys are wearing jumpers. Children use images either as stimulus for a recount or in order to write sentences under each one describing how Rupert is feeling and explaining why.
Plenary. Say, 'Why do you think Oliver Jeffers wrote this book? What does he want us to do in our lives? Why do you think the Hueys react so fiercely towards Rupert when he first wears his new jumper? Do you think they are scared? What message would you give to the Hueys?'
AFL questions. What have I learned today? What made Rupert different? Was it the new jumper or something else?

Table 7.21: Year 3: LI: To be welcoming

Text: *Beegu* (by Alexis Deacon)
Learning intention: To be welcoming
Success criteria. I know the behaviour that makes someone feel like an outsider and I know how to make someone feel welcome.
Starter. Write the word 'outsider' on the board and ask children in pairs to make a list of behaviours and situations that make someone feel like an outsider. Children should then feed back, with you writing up the list on the board to refer to later in the lesson.
Main. Read *Beegu* and discuss what happens in the story. Say, 'How does Beegu feel in the story. [He feels like an outsider.] Why? [People make him feel unwelcome.] How do people make Beegu feel unwelcome? Who makes Beegu welcome in the story? [The children make Beegu feel welcome.] Why do you think the children make Beegu feel welcome? At the end, Beegu says that he will remember the little ones – what does he mean and why does he say that?'
Role play. Say, 'We are going to play the welcoming game.' Send a child out as the detective. While they are gone, identify one child to be the welcoming child. Arrange the children in a circle and ask the detective to come back in. The job for the detective is to find the welcoming child within five guesses. The detective approaches a child and says, 'Hello.' If the child is the welcoming child, they reply, 'Hello! Come and stand with me.' They also move aside in order to let the detective into the circle. However, every other child turns away when approached and ignores the detective.
Activity. Look at the list made at the start of the lesson of behaviours and situations where people are made to feel like an outsider. Children record a behaviour or situation and their response to demonstrate that they know how to stop someone feeling like an outsider and know how to make someone feel welcome.
Plenary. Ask children to feed back some of their responses. Say, 'How do we make sure in our school that there are no outsiders? How do we make sure where we live that there are no outsiders? Every morning when we come to school and meet different people on the playground, do we say, "Good morning!" to everyone? Shall we do that tomorrow?'
AFL questions. What have I learned today? What is one way to be welcoming?

Routledge Taylor & Francis Group

Table 7.22: Year 4: LI: To know when to be assertive

Text: *Dogs Don't Do Ballet* (by Anna Kemp and Sara Ogilvie)
Learning intention: To know when to be assertive
Success criteria. I know what 'assertive' means and I know why being assertive is sometimes hard.
Starter. Write 'pupil voice' on the board. Ask, 'What does it mean? Do we have "pupil voice" at school?' Give examples of demonstration of pupil voice. Say, 'Why is it important to speak up and be heard?'
Main. Read *Dogs Don't Do Ballet*. Say, 'What is the message in the story? How does the dog feel when people say that he can't do ballet? Why do you think people say that? Look at the image on the page near the start where the girl sits on the step. Do you remember the dialogue, "My dog thinks he's a ballerina"? How do you think the girl is feeling? Do you think she loves her dog? Does she try to stop him? What helps to make people change their minds at the end of the story?'
Role play. Say, 'Imagine something you really like doing. How would you feel if people told you that you couldn't do it but gave no explanation as to why?'   Ask for a volunteer to reveal something that they love to do, for example, play football. The child should approach other children in the circle and ask them to play football. Each child replies, 'Don't be silly, children don't play football' or, 'You can't play football; it's not allowed!' At this point the volunteer should not answer back; they should move on to another person.   Repeat four or five times and then ask the volunteer what it feels like to have so many people say that football is not allowed. Say, 'Does it make you want to play regardless or change your behaviour?'   Repeat with different children and different likes.   For the last role play, ask someone to be assertive and reply to the people, saying that the activity is not allowed. Say, 'Is it hard to answer back when everyone disagrees? Can you answer back and keep calm without getting angry or shouting?'
Activity. The children write a letter to the dog giving him advice. If they think that he should give up the ballet then they should tell him so and explain their reasons. If they think that he should continue then they should tell him why and give an explanation. (This could be used as an example of persuasive letter writing.)
Plenary. Ask, 'What does being assertive mean? Is it difficult to stand up for yourself if everyone around you is telling you that you are wrong? Is it easier to just do things people tell you to do so you fit in? Why do some people just fit in without speaking out even if they don't like something? What is the right thing to do? How can we make sure in our school that people are allowed to be who they are without worrying about being different?'
AFL questions. What have I learned today?   What does being assertive mean?

Table 7.23: Year 4: LI: To understand why people choose to get married

Text: *King and King* (by Linda de Hann and Stern Nijland)
Learning intention: To understand why people choose to get married
Success criteria. I know what marriage is and I know who can get married in the UK and I know why people choose to get married.
Starter. Put the word 'marriage' on the board. In pairs, children discuss what it means and what it is for – who gets married and why?
Main. Read and discuss *King and King*. Say, 'Why does the queen want her son to marry a princess? Should he marry a princess in order to please his mum? The prince marries a man in the story – what is the name for this marriage? What does "gay" mean? ['Gay' is when two men love each other or two women love each other – the latter also being known as 'lesbian'.] Does the queen know that her son is gay? Why hasn't he told her? Is she OK about it when he does tell her? Is the queen happy when he gets married to a prince? Why does she shed a tear?'
Role play. Lead a discussion about why people get married. Watch highlights of the royal wedding between William and Kate in 2011 with children making notes on who is getting married, why they are getting married, why they are there so many people watching and how do they think those people are feeling.
Activity. Show an image of a wedding invitation on the board. Children should choose to design a wedding invitation for William and Kate or for the two princes in the story. The invitation is for a royal wedding so it needs to be grand. Ask, 'What information do you need on an invitation?' Make a list first of what is needed.
Plenary. Show some images of marriages, ensuring that there is a mix of genders and ethnicities. Say, 'Some religions say that men and men should not get married. What does the law in the UK say? In 2013 the law was passed by the government to say that a man could marry a man and that a woman could marry a woman. At our school we say there are no outsiders. Does that include people who are gay?' [Yes.]
AFL questions. What have I learned today?   What does British marriage law say?

Table 7.24: Year 4: LI: To overcome language as a barrier

Text: *The Way Back Home* (by Oliver Jeffers)
Learning intention: To overcome language as a barrier
Success criteria. I know that people speak different languages and I know how language can be a barrier and I can find ways to overcome barriers.
Starter. Say, 'What does the learning intention mean? How can language become a barrier to working with someone?' (When you speak a different language from someone it is more difficult to be understood.) In pairs the children should discuss and come up with three ways to make a friend with someone who speaks a different language.
Main. Read and discuss *The Way Back Home*. Say, 'How does the boy feel when he is first stuck on the Moon? When the boy and the Martian hear each other in the dark, why do they think of monsters? The boy and the Martian are very different and they speak different languages but they shake hands. Why? When the boy gets home he could forget about the Martian, why instead does he go back to the Moon? Look at the last page. What is the present? Who has sent it? What do you think happens next?'
Role play. Say, 'Can you make friends with someone when you don't share the same language? Are there other ways to communicate?' Explain that you are going to give the class a task and their job is to complete it without using any language. Tell the children that you want them to stand in a line of height order, tallest to shortest, but no one is allowed to speak. Next, tell the children that you want them to stand in a line of birthday order (or order of house numbers). At the end, discuss how the children managed the task without language. Did anyone help anyone else without having to use words? How?
Activity. Show the page where the boy and the Martian decide what to do. ('Together they thought of ways to fix their machines and how to get them both back home.') Ask, 'What are they saying?' The children should draw a diagram to show how to fix an aeroplane without using any words; they should use arrows and cartoons to show the method.
Plenary. Say, 'Can you make friends with someone if you are different from each other? How do you make friends with someone? What does "body language" mean? When you meet someone for the first time, what effect does a smile have? What effect does a frown have?' Look at the picture of the radio on the last page. Say, 'It is saying, "Hello?" What does that suggest the Martian is beginning to do? How has he learned to say "Hello?"? How do you begin to learn a new language?'
AFL questions. What have I learned today? How can I make friends with someone new?

Ｒ Routledge Taylor & Francis Group

Table 7.25: Year 4: LI: To ask questions

Text: *The Flower* (by John Light)
Learning intention: To ask questions
Success criteria. I know that we all have choices and I know why it's good to learn about new and different things.
Starter. On the board write the word 'questioning'. Say, 'What does it mean to be "questioning"? Is it good to ask questions about how the world works? Why?'
Main. Read *The Flower*. Say, 'Where is the setting for this book? When is it set? What clues are there in the text that the book is set in the future? Describe Brigg's life. Is he a confident person? Why not? How do you know? Why do you think that some books in his library are labelled "dangerous"? How does the flower change Brigg's life? What do you think the flower represents?' [Consider changes in his confidence, difference in a world where everything is the same and feelings of hope.]
Role play. Say, 'In Brigg's world, flowers are not permitted: everything is dull and the same every day. Imagine if Brigg had not smuggled the book out of the library, what would his life be like now? We are going to role play Brigg smuggling the book out of the library. How do you think he felt when he did that?' Identify someone to be a guard; their job is to find the book. Send them out of the room while you give the book to someone playing the role of Brigg and have everyone stand in a circle. Bring back the guard and stand them in the middle of the circle. Give a signal for the smuggling to begin. Brigg passes the book to the next child behind their back and that child passes it on. The guard has four chances to get the book. They should point at a child they think is holding the book and that child should show their hands. If the guard is right then they win. The other children win if they can get the book back to Brigg.
Activity. Put the following phrases on the board for the children to comment on: 'The flower book is labelled dangerous because …' 'Brigg wants to read the book because …' 'The flower makes Brigg feel more confident because …' 'It's good to ask questions and think for yourself because …'
Plenary. Say, 'The place where Brigg lives tells people how to think and how to live. Do you think that people living there are confident or unconfident? Why? What kind of world do we want to live in? Why? How can we make sure that children in our school ask questions and feel confident?'
AFL questions. What have I learned today? Why is it good to learn something new?

Table 7.26: Year 4: LI: To be who you want to be

Text: *Red: A Crayon's Story* (by Michael Hall)
Learning intention: To be who you want to be
Success criteria. I know why people sometimes don't speak up and I know everyone in my school should be proud of who they are.
Starter. Say, 'With a partner make a list of as many colours as you can.' Establish who in the class has the most.
Main. Read and discuss *Red: A Crayon's Story*. Say, 'What did the red crayon find difficult? What made everyone think he was red? What colour was he inside? How did other characters try to help him become red? Make a list of advice from different characters – mum, teacher and grandparents. Why did his grandparents give him a red scarf and not a blue scarf?'
Role play. Give nine children flash cards with lines from the book where 'everyone seemed to have something to say' (see above).   Identify a child to be Red and give them a red cape to wrap around them. Now explain that Red keeps doing blue things. Say, 'Let's hear what everyone around him is saying.' Ask Red to stand in the middle of the circle and have each child with a flash card approach and read out their line.   At the end, ask children how Red is feeling and whether the lines in the book were helpful in increasing his confidence.   Now ask everyone to think of a different line to say to Red to make him feel confident again. Ask children to approach Red and say their new lines to make him feel confident again.
Activity. The children should draw Red in his red cover and write their new advice for him. Say, 'Should he continue trying to be red? Why? Why not?'
Plenary. Say, 'Who in the story changes everything for Red?' (The Berry crayon changes everything for Red when he asks him to make a blue ocean.) Say, 'How do you think that changed Red's life? Look at what his mum says on the last page. (Olive says, "My son is brilliant!") How do you think that makes Red feel? At the end he seems to change his name – why? Does Blue now feel accepted and proud? Why? How can we make sure at our school that everyone feels proud to be who they are?'
AFL questions. What have I learned today?   Why does Red change his name to Blue?

Table 7.27: Year 5: LI: To learn from our past

Text: *Where the Poppies Now Grow* (by Hilary Robinson and Martin Impey)
Learning intention: To learn from our past
Success criteria. I know why people fight in wars and I know Britain fought in two World Wars, and I know why we remember those who died in the First World War and Second World War.
Starter. Say, 'When was the First World War and when was the Second World War? How old would a person who was aged 18 at the start of the First World War be now? How about an 18 year-old from the start of the Second World War? In the First World War, trenches were used in fighting. What was a trench? How did they work? Why did so many soldiers die while they fought in the trenches?'
Main. Read *Where the Poppies Now Grow*. Say, 'How did the boys feel about war before they went to fight? How did they feel when they were there? Why do you think Ben was left to die in the field? Was it because no one cared or for another reason? [It was about fear and because others thought that he was dead.] How old are Ben and Ray now? How do you think they feel now about the war? Why are they saluting in a field of poppies? Why don't they just forget about the past?'
Role play. Ask an elderly person to visit the class to be interviewed by the children about events in their life. It does not have to be a person who fought in a war; everyone will have a story to tell about how times were different, for example, the way schools were 50 years ago, or the way families lived. Ask the person if they knew of anyone who fought in a war and how the war affected them. Ask if they think it is important to remember what happened a long time ago. Ask the class, 'Why is it important not to forget?' Put the children in small groups and ask each group to ask a question about the past. For example: 'What were your hopes when you were young?', 'What are you proud of?', 'What were the good times for you and the difficult times?', 'If you could go back, would you do anything differently?' and 'What message would you like to give young people today about growing up?'
Activity. There are many photographs available on the internet showing veterans on parade or in services. Children should record questions they would like to ask veterans about their experiences.
Plenary. Say, 'How do we remember people who fought in wars today? Why is the poppy used? Each year there are less and less soldiers attending Remembrance services for the two World Wars – why is this? Do you think we should continue to hold Remembrance services when there are no soldiers left? Why?'
AFL questions. What have I learned today? Why do we use the poppy every year in Britain to remember people who fought in wars? What sorts of things can we learn when talking to people who have been alive for a long time?

Table 7.28: Year 5: LI: To justify my actions

Text: *Rose Blanche* (by Ian McEwan and Roberto Innocenti)
Learning intention: To justify my actions
Success criteria. I know that sometimes we have to make difficult decisions and I can justify my actions.
Starter. Show an image of Jewish children in the Second World War. Ask, 'What is happening in the picture? Why? Who were the Nazis? How did the Nazis justify their actions at the time?'
Main. Read *Rose Blanche*. Say, 'How do you know the book is told from a child's perspective? Where are the lorries in the story going? What are they carrying? Why?' Explain that concentration camps were set up in the Second World War in Germany and Poland to remove people who were Jewish and also any people who were different from the Nazis (such as disabled and gay people and anyone who disagreed with the Nazis). Tell the children that millions of people were killed. Say, 'What does Rose do in the story? Why does she do that? How do you think her mother would have felt if she found out? What would the soldiers do to Rose and her family if they found out? What happens to Rose at the end of the story? Look at the language in the last paragraph: "Fresh grasses advanced across the land. There were new explosions of colour. Trees put on their bright new uniforms." What does the author want to convey through the use of this language?'
Role play. Put the children in pairs. One is Mum and one is Rose. Mum has found out that Rose is taking food to the children in the concentration camp and is waiting for her when she gets back one day. Role play the conversation between Mum and Rose. Rose should justify why she is doing that. How does Mum feel?
Activity. Say, 'Rose's actions are very brave. Why does she risk her life to do what she does?' The children should write a letter from Rose to a friend explaining what she has discovered and how it makes her feel. The letter should contain a description of what she has chosen to do and why.
Plenary. Say, 'If Rose had written a letter describing her actions in Nazi Germany what would have happened? In the prison what was the effect on the prisoners of Rose's kindness? Did she do the right thing? How can we make sure that situations like this never happen again where we live?'
AFL questions. What have I learned today? Was Rose right to do what she did or was Rose wrong to do what she did? What reasons can be given to justify this opinion?

Ⓡ Routledge Taylor & Francis Group

Table 7.29: Year 5: LI: To recognise when someone needs help

Text: *How to Heal a Broken Wing* (by Bob Graham)
Learning intention: To recognise when someone needs help
Success criteria. I know that people have different life experiences and I can empathise with others.
Starter. Put the word 'empathy' on the board. The children should work in pairs to come up with a definition.
Main. Read *How to Heal a Broken Wing*. The children should discuss in talk partners what they believe to be the themes in the story and feed back. Once everyone has fed back, read the postscript at the end about Amnesty International. Partners should then talk again about what they think the book may be about. Explain that Amnesty International helps people around the world who are in prison because they speak up about wanting freedom of speech and democracy. Discuss the meaning of these terms. Explain that in the UK we have freedom of speech and democracy but in some countries people are not allowed to vote or disagree with the government. Amnesty helps people who are in prison and can't tell their story, by speaking up for them. Read the book again and ask the children to think about what the bird represents. Ask the children what 'No one looked' means. Say, 'Why didn't the bird ask for help from the people around it? [Because it had no voice, so the boy stopped and spoke up for it.] If the boy had walked on, what would have happened to the bird? What was the effect on the bird when the boy stopped and helped?
Role play. Give out sum cards to the children. (Each card has one sum on it, and most are easily solved mentally, but one or two are more difficult, for example, 457×36.) No one should show their card to anyone else. Explain that most of the sums are easy to work out inside people's heads, and we are going to go around the circle saying the sum and the answer. Say, 'If you are not sure of your answer then you need to think about your options. You could say, "I can't do it" or you could say, "I'm not doing it" or you could ask for help when it is your turn.' Make the point that if someone gets a sum wrong we should not be laughing at them but rather be helping them. You will be looking to see who gives one another respect. Go around the circle and ask children to give their answers. When you get to the child with the most difficult sum, praise children who help or offer solutions. (You could have several difficult cards.)
Activity. There are many pages in the book with no words. Select one such page and ask children to write a descriptive piece about the image. Encourage the use of feelings and emotion words.

Routledge Taylor & Francis Group

Table 7.29 (continued)

Plenary. Say, 'How did the role play feel? How did it feel to have an easy sum? How did it feel to have a difficult sum? Were you worried about how people may react when you couldn't do the sum? How would you have felt if no one had offered help? If you see that someone needs help, what can you do? Why may they not ask for help? How can we make sure in our class that everyone knows it is OK to ask for help?'

Return to the definition of 'empathy'. Ask, 'Do we want to change this definition?

AFL questions. What have I learned today?
What can I do if I think that someone needs help?
What does 'empathy' mean?

Table 7.30: Year 5: LI: To appreciate artistic freedom

Text: *The Artist Who Painted a Blue Horse* (by Eric Carle)
Learning intention: To appreciate artistic freedom
Success criterion. I know that art can demonstrate freedom.
Starter. Discuss the learning intention. Look at paintings by Franz Marc. In pairs, the children should describe what they see and what is different about the paintings. Ask, 'How would you describe the style of Franz Marc?'
Main. Read *The Artist Who Painted a Blue Horse* and discuss the pictures. Ask, 'What is different about the pictures?' Read the text at the end of the book about Franz Marc, Eric Carle and Herr Krauss. Say, 'Who were the Nazis? The Nazis believed the opposite to what we say in our school – why? What would have happened to Herr Krauss if the Nazis had found out he showed Eric the paintings? Would the Nazis have allowed us to teach using books like *The Artist Who Painted a Blue Horse*? Why do you think Herr Krauss showed the paintings?'
Role play. Visit Reception class to paint different animals with the children there. Say, 'We are going to remember Herr Krauss in our lesson and make his teaching live on. We are going to encourage young children to express themselves freely using different colours.'
Activity. Say, 'The Nazis wanted to stop children in schools talking about difference and diversity and freedom of expression. What things do we do in our school to make sure that the Nazi ideas never happen again? Make a list, justify why we do these things and what is the impact on the children in our school.' *Or:* Say, 'Write an account of what you did in the Reception class. Think about why it was important. Do you think you made a difference? How? How can we make sure the young children in our school continue to feel free in their expression?'
Plenary. Say, 'Why is it important to encourage young children to express themselves freely? Is a good imagination important? Why? Did the Nazis want people to express themselves or to question things? Why not? How do we make sure that Nazis never come to power again? Why do you think we talk so much about "no outsiders" in our school?'
AFL questions. What have I learned today? What have we learned about today? What would I say to Franz Marc if I could travel back in time and meet him?

Table 7.31: Year 5: LI: To accept people who are different from me

Text: *And Tango Makes Three* (by Justin Richardson and Peter Parnell)
Learning intention: To accept people who are different from me
Success criteria. I know that there are different people living in my community and I accept everyone who is different from me.
Starter. In groups, children discuss how different animals live – on their own, in pairs or in groups.
Main. Read *And Tango Makes Three* apart from the author note at the end. Say, 'What makes Mr Gramzay think that Roy and Silo are in love? What is the word when two men are in a relationship like Roy and Silo? (gay) What is the name for two women in a relationship like that of Roy and Silo? (lesbian) When Mr Gramzay gave Roy and Silo an egg, did they look after it properly? Were they good dads? How do we know?'
Role play. Give out 'snap' playing cards showing animal pairs. Explain to the children that they should not show anyone their card. Keep one card back so that someone will not find a pair. Say to the children that their task is to find their animal pair but they cannot speak; they have to move or make noises like their animal. Set the children off with the understanding that, as they find their partner, they should sit down together so that by the end there is a solitary animal left with no partner. At the end, ask, 'What we can do with this lonely animal?' If no one offers to take them in without prompting then ask if an established pair will allow this animal to join their family. Reinforce to the children that families are all different, so if a duck wants to live with a penguin then that's OK!
Activity. There are many stories on the internet about gay animals in zoos. Look up the story of two gay vultures in Alwetterzoo, Munich, Germany who were separated by the keeper in 2010. Use the quote from the curator: 'They weren't happy as a gay couple anyway. The other vultures picked on them and stole their nest materials.' Discuss this quote. Ask, 'What would be a better response from the zoo?' The children should write a letter to the zoo giving advice.
Plenary. *And Tango Makes Three* is a true story – read the author note. Ask, 'Do any of the other penguins bully Roy and Silo for being gay? What does that say about the penguins and the zoo? How can we make sure that gay or lesbian people feel welcome in our school?'
AFL question. What have I learned today?

Table 7.32: Year 6: LI: To promote diversity

Text: *My Princess Boy* (Cheryl Kilodavis and Suzanne DeSimone)
Learning intention: To promote diversity
Success criteria. I know what diversity is and I can accept that other people may be different from me and I understand that living in the UK means accepting and celebrating diversity.
Starter. Discuss the learning intention and the success criteria. The children should provide examples of diversity and the ways in which our school promotes and celebrates diversity.
Main. Read and discuss *My Princess Boy*. Say, 'In the book what upsets Princess Boy? Is he hurting anyone by wearing a dress? Does it really matter? Who loves Princess Boy in the story? How do you know? Do you think that Princess Boy feels like a girl, or does he just want to wear a dress?' [We don't know the answer to this question; the important thing is not to judge him and to accept him whatever he wears or wants to be.]
Role play. There are interviews available on the internet of one author of the book, Cheryl Kilodavis, talking about her son, Dyson, on US television. The story is a true one and this is the boy in the book. While watching, ask the children to make notes on:
What did Mum and Dad think when Dyson first wanted to wear a dress?
Does Dyson want to be a boy or a girl?
What happened at school?
What is Dyson's response to teasing?
What arguments does Mum have to support her son?
Who helped Mum to make up her mind about what to do? What did they say?
Do you think the interviewer is listening to Mum?
Plenary. Say, 'If Dyson came to our school would he be welcome? What can we do every day at our school to make sure that children like Dyson feel welcome? What does British law say about gender identity?' Refer to the seven characteristics on the Equality Act poster. Say, 'Which characteristic is relevant to this story?' (Gender identity) Ask, 'How can we make sure that we are following the law at our school?'
AFL questions. What have I learned today? How could Dyson be made to feel welcome if he came to our school? For additional specific lesson plans and picture books about Transgender awareness go to www.equalitiesprimary.com.

Table 7.33: Year 6: LI: To stand up to discrimination

Text: *The Whisperer* (by Nick Butterworth)
Learning intention: To stand up to discrimination
Success criteria. I understand the reasons why some people may choose to hide their identity and I understand how people are labelled by rumours and assumptions and I can identify ways to stand up to prejudice and challenge rumours.
Starter. Define 'discrimination'. The children should give examples of how a person can suffer discrimination.
Main. Read and discuss *The Whisperer*. Say, 'When the parents told Monty and Amber to leave each other, what do you think they should have done? Did they do the right thing? What is a rumour? Why does the rat say, "Better than a letter, better than anything, everybody hears the whisper but they don't see the whisperer!"? What does he mean? How does the rumour affect Amber and Monty? What changes attitudes for Amber and Monty when they return? (Tiger) What do you think of the ending? Is there a message in this book?'
Role play. Show the children a pile of cards and explain that they are all blank except one, which has a cross on it. Give out the cards while you are talking and tell the children they must not show anyone their card. If you have the card with the cross on it then the object of the game for you is to have no one find out. If you have a blank card then the object of the game for you is to find out who has the cross.   Give the children five minutes to mingle and find out who has the cross. They should simply ask people if they have the cross. Everyone will say that they don't have it but one person will be lying. Can they work out who is that person? Remind the children that they must not show their card to anyone.   After five minutes, sit the children in a circle and say that you want each of them to reveal who they think has the cross. The person who does have the cross at this stage will have to lie again and say that it is someone else. Go around the circle so that everyone gets to name someone. When children nominate a name, ask them to give their reason for thinking that it's that person.   When everyone has named someone, go around the circle again and this time ask the children one at a time to reveal their card and say whether they had the cross or not.   Did the person with the cross manage to remain hidden?
Post-role-play discussion. How did the person with the cross feel about having to lie to everybody?   If people were nominated while in the circle at the end how did that feel?   Did anyone hear any rumours during the game about who might have the cross?   Did the person who had the cross spread any rumours and, if so, why did they do that? (To deflect attention.)

Ｒ Routledge Taylor & Francis Group

Ask, 'Can you think of any circumstances in real life where this situation may happen? When do people sometimes hide their identity? For example, if someone was gay do you think they would tell everyone? Why not? Why do some gay people sometimes hide the fact that they are gay? What can we do about this in our school? If someone in our school said they were gay, do you think they would be welcomed? How can we make sure in our school that no one feels they have to hide who they are?'

Plenary. Ask, 'What is the Equality Act 2010? How is it relevant to our school? What are the seven characteristics? How can we make sure that everyone feels welcome at our school?'

AFL questions. What have I learned today?
Why are all people welcome in our school?
Why does it not matter if you are … (choose one of the characteristics in the Equality Act 2010) at our school?

Ⓡ Routledge
Taylor & Francis Group

Table 7.34: Year 6: LI: To challenge the causes of racism

Text: *The Island* (by Armin Greder)
Learning intention: To challenge the causes of racism
Starter. Write the word 'racism' on the board. The children in pairs should draw a mind map and discuss what 'racism' is or what is the cause of 'racism'. Feed back ideas to the class.
Success criteria. I know what prejudice is and I know what can happen if racism is not challenged and I know how to challenge racist behaviour.
Main. Read *The Island*. Say, 'Describe the character of the man washed up on the beach. What is the reaction of the people on the island? On one of the early pages there is an image of children pointing sticks at another child. What are they doing? Why? Why didn't the man stay in the goat pen? Everyone gave a reason why the man couldn't work with them. Why? List the rumours that were spread about the man. Why do you think he eats bones with his hands? What is the role of the fisherman? What happened to him as a result? What do you think happens to the man at the end? Why do the people build a wall? Is there a message in this story? What is it?'
Role play. Say, 'We are going to concentrate on the role of the fisherman.' On each table give out cards – half of which should be blank and half should have an image of a fish on them. Children with a fish card take on the role of the fisherman whose job it is to stand up for the man. The other children in the group should use the arguments listed in the book. Can the fishermen convince anyone? Ask some of the fishermen to feed back to the class some of their arguments and how it felt to stand up for the man.
Activity. Draw a cartoon strip telling the story of *The Island*. Limit your cartoons to six images. The children should ensure that they include the main features of the story. Include language from the book.
Plenary. Talk about the wall built around the island. Say, 'What will be the consequence of having a wall? (The people will never meet anyone different from them.) How will that affect their lives? Where does racism come from? Will the wall help or hinder the people to overcome racism? Have you heard any racist comments in our school? How can you respond if you hear comments based on prejudice? What does our school say about racist behaviour?'
AFL questions. What have I learned today? When does racism happen?

Table 7.35: Year 6: LI: To consider how my life may change as I grow up

Text: *Love You Forever* (by Robert Munsch)
Learning intention: To consider how my life may change as I grow up
Success criteria. I know that we all grow old and I understand the cycle of life.
Starter. Ask the children in groups to identify the main life stages. Start with being a baby. Ask, 'What is the next life stage? How do we change?'
Main. Read *Love You Forever*. Ask, 'How does the mother feel towards her son? Do her feelings change as he grows up? How does she feel when he is being difficult as he grows up? How do you think her son feels when she sings the song? What do you think about the end of the story? Why does the man sing the song to his daughter? Is there a message in this story?' In talk partners, the children should discuss what the message in this story is and give examples to justify their responses.
Activity. The children should compile a time line for an imaginary person to show how they change in their life. Ask, 'What sort of life events may happen? Do they love anyone? Get married? Stay single? Have children?'
Plenary. Ask, 'Why do you think the author wrote this book? The story is called "Love you forever". Is love for ever? Can people change whom they love? As we grow older, how do you think we change?'
AFL questions. What have we learned today? What do you want to achieve in your lifetime?

Table 7.36: Year 6: LI: To recognise my freedom

Text: *Dreams of Freedom* (by Amnesty International)
Learning intention: To recognise my freedom
Success criteria. I know I have rights and I know that I can decide how I live my life when I grow up and I know I can be what and who I want to be.
Starter. Say, 'What are the rights of a child? Does anyone know what the Universal Declaration of Human Rights (UDHR) is? Why was it written? For whom?'
Main. Read *Dreams of Freedom*. Ask, 'Why do you think the author wrote the book? Did any pages stand out for you? Any images? What do you think is the key message in the text?'
Role play. Give children the quote from Chief Standing Bear of the Ponica Tribe: 'My hand is not the colour of yours. But if I pierce it, I shall feel pain. If you pierce your hand, you shall also feel pain. The blood that will flow from mine will be the same colour as yours. I am a man. The same god made us both.'   Or the quote from Aung San Suu Kyi: 'The only real prison is fear and the only real freedom is freedom from fear. You should never let your fears prevent you from doing what you know is right.'   Or the quote from the presenter and journalist Clare Balding: 'If I am different I make no apology and I hope that others will have the courage to be themselves and stand up for what they believe in, [and] fight for those who need protection [and] love who they want to love and be proud of it.'   In groups, children discuss the quotes and what their meanings are. Prepare a response to read to the class giving explanations and examples of how the quotes affect us in school and in our life.
Activity. Show the image for the first page: 'Freedom to dream, to achieve great things, we must dream as well as do'. The children should make their own posters to illustrate the quote by Anatloe France. They should draw themselves in a group showing what their dreams are.
Plenary. Ask, 'If you were asked to contribute a quote for *Dreams of Freedom*, what would you write?' The children should write their own quotes and read them out to the class if they wish.
AFL questions. What have I learned today?   What are my dreams?   What would my quote for *Dreams of Freedom* be?

Appendix

Below is a reproduction of a letter to the parents of children attending Parkfield Community School inviting them to look at the books we were using to teach about challenging homophobia. The lesson plans we were using at the time were known as Challenging Homophobia in Primary Schools (CHIPS). Some of the books and lesson plans are featured in this resource (Chapter 7). This letter followed a number of complaints to the school about the lesson plans. Each year group had their own meeting.

Dear Parents/Carers

I understand a small number of parents have been asking recently about the way the school is fulfilling our statutory duty to promote diversity and support British Law, in particular the Equality Act and challenging homophobia.

At Parkfield Community School we listen to our parents and welcome feedback, while at the same time following guidance from the government on how to teach British Values. We did invite all parents to look at the CHIPS (Challenging Homophobia In Primary Schools) books back in September. If anyone however missed that or would like to see the books again, we will be giving parents in each class an opportunity to look at the books for their year group over the next few weeks.

Your meeting will take place from **2:40-3.00**. Please enter school through the main reception. The meeting will give parents another opportunity to look at the books for their year group and ask any questions about our work on diversity and difference.
Please come on the date that is set aside for your class group, so you can speak with your class teacher. The date for Year 4 parents is:

Friday 17th April 2:40-3:00

CHIPS is currently being rolled out to *every* primary school in Birmingham, and to schools in many other cities around the UK. Parkfield children must not be left behind; we look forward to working with you to make this a success at our school.

Yours sincerely

R Routledge
Taylor & Francis Group

References

Amnesty International (2015) *Dreams of Freedom*, Frances Lincoln Children's Books, London.

Battram S (2005) *Dougal's Deep Sea Diary*, Templar Publishing, Dorking.

Biddulph R (2015) *Blown Away*, HarperCollins, London.

Brownlow M & Rickerty S (2014) *Ten Little Pirates*, Orchard Books, London.

Butterworth N (1991) *My Grandpa Is Amazing*, Walker Books, London.

Butterworth N (2004) *The Whisperer*, HarperCollins Children's Books, London.

Carle E (2011) *The Artist Who Painted a Blue Horse*, Puffin Books, London.

Dathan M (2015) 'General election 2015: school visit backfires for Labour's Tristram Hunt as kid says he'd vote Ukip "to get all the foreigners out"', *The Independent*, 16 April, online, www.independent.co.uk/news/uk/politics/generalelection/general-election-2015-school-visit-backfires-for-labours-tristram-hunt-as-kid-says-hed-vote-ukip-to-get-all-the-foreigners-out-10181500.html (accessed May 2015).

De Hann L & Nijland S (2002) *King and King*, Tricycle Press, Berkeley.

Deacon A (2003) *Beegu*, Random House, London.

Department for Education (2011) 'Teachers' Standards', Department for Education, 1 July, online, www.gov.uk/government/publications/teachers-standards (accessed July 2015).

Dodd L (2006) *The Other Ark*, Puffin, London.

Elliot R (2010) *Just Because*, Lion Children's Books, Oxford.

Government (2010) *Equality Act 2010*, online, www.legislation.gov.uk (accessed July 2015).

Government Equalities Office (2013) 'Equality Act 2010: Guidance', GOV.UK, 27 February, online, www.gov.uk/equality-act-2010-guidanceauthor (accessed June 2015).

Graham B (2010) *How to Heal a Broken Wing*, Walker, London.

Gravett E (2010) *Blue Chameleon*, Macmillan, London.

Gravett E (2011) *The Odd Egg*, Macmillan, New York.

Greder A (2007) *The Island*, Allen & Unwin, NSW.

Hall M (2015) *Red: A Crayon's Story*, HarperCollins Children's Books, New York.

Heap S & Sharratt N (2003) *Red Rockets and Rainbow Jelly*, Puffin Books, London.

Hoffman M & Asquith R (2010) *The Great Big Book of Families*, Frances Lincoln Children's books, London.

Jeffers O (2008) *The Way Back Home*, HarperCollins, London.

Jeffers O (2012) *The Hueys in the New Jumper*, HarperCollins Children's Books, London.

Kemp A & Ogilvie S (2010) *Dogs Don't Do Ballet*, Simon & Schuster, London.

Kilodavis C & DeSimone S (2009) *My Princess Boy*, Aladdin, Simon & Schuster Publishing, New York.

Light J (2006) *The Flower*, Child's Play, Swindon.

McEwan I & Innocenti R (2004) *Rose Blanche*, Random House, London.

McKee D (1989) *Elmer*, Andersen Press, London.

McKee D (2009) *Two Monsters*, Andersen Press, London.

Moffat A (2007) *Challenging Homophobia in Primary Schools: An Early Years Resource*, Hounslow Healthy Schools, London.

Moffat A (2012) *Behaviour, Safety and Well Being: 100+ Lesson Plans for the Primary Classroom*, Speechmark Publishing, Milton Keynes.

Moffat A (2015) *Equalities Primary*, online, www.equalitiesprimary.com (accessed July 2015).

Munsch R (1986) *Love You Forever*, Firefly Books, Ontario.

Newman L & Thompson C (2009) *Mommy Mama & Me*, Tricycle Press, Berkeley.

No Outsiders Project Team (2010) *Undoing Homophobia in Primary Schools*, Trentham Books Ltd, Stoke-on-Trent.

Parr T (2003) *The Family Book*, Little Brown Books, New York.

Parr T (2009) *It's Okay to Be Different*, Little Brown, London.

Richardson J & Parnell P (2015) *And Tango Makes Three*, Little Simon, London.

Robinson H & Impey M (2014) *Where the Poppies Now Grow*, Strauss House Productions, York

.

Rosen M (2007) *This Is Our House*, Walker Books Ltd, London.

Sharratt N & Goodheart P (2004) *You Choose*, Corgi Childrens, London.

Sharratt N & Goodheart P (2004) *Red Rockets and Rainbow Jelly*, Puffin, London.

Sif B (2012) *Oliver*, Walker Books, London.

Stockdale S, Strick A & Asquith R (2010) *Max the Champion*, Frances Lincoln Children's Books, London.

Velthujis M (1995) *Frog and the Stranger*, Andersen Press, London.

Vyner T (2002) *World Team*, Red Fox Publishing, London.

Walsh M (2004) *My World, Your World*, Random House, London.

Willis J (2015) *The First Slodge*, Little Tiger Press, London.